THEY HARVEST DESPAIR

THEY HARVEST DESPAIR

The Migrant Farm Worker

by Dale Wright

Foreword by Senator Harrison A. Williams, Jr., of New Jersey

Beacon Press Boston

Library of Congress catalogue card number: 65-13532

Published simultaneously in Canada by Saunders of Toronto, Ltd.

Printed in the United States of America

The illustrations are from photographs by Dick DeMarsico and are used by permission of the *New York World-Telegram & Sun*.

The author wishes to acknowledge his indebtedness to Miss Fay Bennett, Norton Mockridge, Woody Klein, Samuel Singletary, James E. Hudson, Robert Prall, Allan Keller, and Wesley First.

To Dolores
Whose patience has been
strengthening and inspiring

Foreword

One of the hardest tasks facing those who have wanted to do something about the shocking living and working conditions of the migrant farm worker has been to make the public aware that the migrant worker and his problems even exist in prosperous twentieth century America. The vast majority have had little idea of the conditions under which their fruits and vegetables have been harvested. The migrant worker has lived out his life, ignored, forgotten, and left behind by progress. Although church groups, humanitarian organizations, and labor unions have been working hard to help the migrant, only an aroused public can bring about the legislative action necessary to eliminate the national disgrace of the migrant way of life. Without labor unions or leadership of their own, the migrant workers have been a voiceless and voteless minority of poverty. But in the reporting of Dale Wright, the migrant has found an eloquent and hard-hitting spokesman. Written from his bitter experience, Dale Wright's reports of the life of the migrant won well deserved awards when they first appeared in the *New York World-Telegram and Sun.*

As one who read and admired the original series, I am glad that he has expanded his vivid account into a book. With the objectivity and accuracy of a trained reporter, Dale Wright makes plain the human tragedy behind the statistics, and his anger at the human waste and hardship bound up in the term "migrant farm worker" is apparent and justified.

It is unfortunate but true that many of the facts found by Mr. Wright on his 1961 trip remain unchanged in 1964. But thanks to his work and that of others, important progress has been made on behalf of the migrant and his family. In 1962, Congress passed a Migrant Health Act which provided funds to the states to operate clinics for migrant workers. Last year migrant programs were included in the Economic Opportunity Act and the Housing Act. A law requiring the registration of crew leaders is now on the books. This measure can be an effective weapon in doing away with the worst abuses of crew leaders which Mr. Wright so graphically describes in this book.

Much remains to be done before the migrant worker can take his place as a full-fledged American citizen. The migrant worker is still denied the economic rights of collective bargaining privileges and a minimum wage which are guaranteed by law to workers in almost every major industry, and he still lacks access to adequate housing, education, and medical care for his family. As we in the Congress work to improve existing legislation and to enact new and needed laws, Mr. Wright's book will serve to alert the public to the continuing need for further action. It is heartening to know that courageous reporters like Mr. Wright still serve as active gadflies to America's conscience. His human and moving plea for migrants should be widely read by every American who believes that the American dream of a better life should become a reality for all our citizens.

HARRISON A. WILLIAMS, JR.

United States Senate

Preface

The migrant farm worker in America has been studied, surveyed, investigated, microscoped, and diagnosed over the years as the sickest, most depressed, yet least-known member of the nation's work force.

As the seasons change and fruits, berries, and vegetables ripen for gathering, the itinerant harvester moves along from one crop to another across county and state lines, often with the sum total of his earthly possessions in a shopping bag or a canned-goods carton. Caught up in the ebb and flow of the migrant stream, he—and sometimes his family—often travel long distances to and from the place of labor. For reasons of birth, because of color or national origin, or because of lack of skills and/or education which could equip him for other employment, he all too often never escapes.

As a staff writer for Scripps-Howard's New York *World-Telegram and Sun,* I took a long, hard, painstaking look at the migrant farm worker along the Atlantic seaboard during the spring, summer and early fall of 1961. I left the cavernous, humming city room in downtown Manhattan in April of that year and traveled—in the air-conditioned comfort of a jet airliner—to Florida, where I moved into the mainstream of the migrant flow heading northward. At intervals during the succeeding six months—well into October—I lived, worked, ate, and more than once suffered with crews of transient harvesters on long journeys that ended in the rich, black vegetable fields of Eastern Long Island.

The migrant farm workers I knew best harvest the fields in the Atlantic Coast states. They are for the most part native-born Negroes from the Deep South—Florida, Georgia, Alabama, the Carolinas, and some from Mississippi and Texas. But I also traveled and worked with off-shore Puerto Ricans, West Indians, Mexicans, Bahamians, and a scattering of Anglo-American whites. They begin their seasonal journeys in late January or early February with south Florida citrus crops, then move from field to field, through tomatoes and potatoes in Florida; corn, snap beans, and cucumbers in the Carolinas; berries and fruits in Virginia and Maryland; then perhaps vegetable crops again in Delaware, New Jersey, and New York. Many follow the crops into northern New England and Canada, where, in late November and early December, they help bring in another potato harvest.

When the last of these crops have been harvested, it is back again to the Deep South where the cycle starts over again. All of these workers, no matter what their origin, no matter what the color of their skin, have one thing in common: they are a miserable, forgotten lot. Few really care about them; most would prefer to ignore them.

Once the crops are in and packaged in baskets, or bound up in bags, or bottled and canned at the processors', there is no further need for the hand harvester and the women and children he brought along with him on the bus or truck or broken-down automobile that labored up the road. He is unwanted in the farm community which purchased his labor so cheaply; he is a misfit, often a burden on the urban center nearby. He is inarticulate, the possessor of few skills, disorganized, rootless; and because of his migrancy and the accident of his birth as a Negro, a Puerto Rican, a Mexican or West Indian, he is a minority within a minority.

After exhaustive research on the subject of migrant farm workers along the East Coast, I assembled what is believed to be one of the first detailed reports on the "stoop worker"—from the inside looking out.

I was vacationing in Puerto Rico when fire swept the squalid quarters which housed potato-field workers near Cutchogue, Long Island, and the newspaper's editors agreed that it was time to let the articles begin.

The series of ten installments created a national furor. They were twice reprinted in the *Congressional Record*—by New York Representatives John V. Lindsay and William Fitts Ryan. In addition they were reprinted in pamphlet form by the tens of thousands by three social-service agencies interested in improving the lot of the migratory agricultural laborer. The articles were also cited by the American Newspaper Guild as one of the two most distinguished pieces of reporting for 1961 in the United States or Canada and I won one of two Heywood Broun Memorial Awards for that year. It is the highest distinction bestowed annually by the American Newspaper Guild, of which the late Mr. Broun was a founder. Other national journalism prizes for the series included the Public Service Award of the Society of The Silurians (an organization of twenty-five-year New York City newspapermen) and the Paul Tobenkin Award, named for the late New York *Herald Tribune* reporter who became famous for public service and socially oriented newswriting. The articles were also nominated by the *New York World-Telegram and Sun* for the 1962 Pulitzer Prize as the most meritorious national reporting for the prior year.

The states of New York and New Jersey both have re-examined and reorganized their migrant farm-labor programs to some extent as a result of these newspaper articles, and have taken remedial action. In New York, for example, the State Labor Department set up pilot programs in areas of heavy farm-labor concentration. Teams of experts were sent to acquaint the workers with their rights and privileges under the law—as well as with their responsibilities while resident in the state. The program, greatly expanded, has become part of the Department's permanent services for migrants.

This report is the migrant's own story—a story that needs telling. It presents no sociological cause-and-effect studies. It offers no clinical analyses. It deals only briefly in statistics. It has none of the flavor of do-gooder philosophizing. All these are already in the record as a part of the monumental documentation on the plight of the transient harvester. This report is, rather, an amplification of the migrant's own faint cries—sometimes through the voices of his children—from the shadowy, bewildering microcosm where he lives out there beyond the trees that hide his dwelling from sight. They are cries of bitterness, resentment, unhappiness, the futility of existence cut off from the rest of humanity. I know that bitterness, that resentment, that seemingly insurmountable futility, because I lived and labored alongside the migrant farm worker.

D.W.

Contents

THEY HARVEST DESPAIR

1

Flecks of Red in the Dirt

Red stood erect beside me in the long row. Before him stretched a mile and a half of tomatoes yet to be gathered. Behind him, reaching back to the bordering pine trees, lay another mile and a half already picked clean. It was the "last pick" of the fields and the vegetables were red ripe and rotting on the vines. Gnats and flies and other assorted arthropoda buzzed around the spoiling tomatoes and got in the way. Keeping the bugs away from your face and out of your eyes was an irksome, wearying task.

It was just after midday. The sun was almost straight up, and the sky was a faded, cloudless blue. From the Florida Keys toward the southeast, a damp, muggy breeze blustered across the vast fields. The acrid, pungent odor of the insecticide that had been machine-sprayed over the crops hung flaccidly in the folds of the hot April winds. The irregular waves of the breeze brought Red little relief; and the rest of the harvesters who toiled along with him were rather less than comfortable. The winds stirred whirls of dust and leaves and other flotsam between the rows of tomatoes, then they died out listlessly, in the perimeter of pines around the field. Sometimes the winds came in spurts strong enough to dash the red dirt into your face, inside your shirt collar, and down the back of your neck. Sometimes you thought about these petty annoyances—the bugs and the dirt and the sweat—but most of the time it was the work that bothered you, the labor of gathering the red ripe tomatoes into the baskets, then toting the heavy burdens to the end of the row.

A battered pickup truck sped down a dirt road along one side of the field, a wake of red dust close behind it. Three parallel white streaks in the sky to the north were evidence that a tiny squadron of jet aircraft was carrying out its secret assignment in its own unfathomable way. The planes were so high in the sky that the sound of their engines was just a faint buzz, not much louder than the flies and gnats. You speculated that the pilots were en route from their home base nearby to an important rendezvous somewhere. You knew that the men who sat at the instrument panels had not the slightest knowledge of or concern for the miserable, sweating, complaining stooped-over humanity thousands of feet below—*their* only assignment to gather tomatoes out of these fields—*their* only rendezvous another field somewhere up the road.

The heat was oppressive. It fell down over my shoulders and across my back like a wet, steaming blanket. It wormed its way under my T shirt and into the creases of my boxer short underwear. Salt sweat trickled off my forehead in streaks and seeped into my eyes, making them smart and tear. The taste of the salt droplets on my lips was not unpleasant, but mixed with the grime from the fields, they formed a film on my face and neck, on my hands and arms.

All around me, and all around Red, whose long row adjoined mine, the 200-odd hand harvesters squatted and crawled along the straight rows, pushing or dragging their baskets. The pickers—all sizes, both sexes—ranged in age from the early teens well up through Social Security retirement years. The baskets when heaping full held five-eighths of a bushel and weighed 30 to 40 pounds each. Some of the women and the younger boys and girls had difficulty managing the heavy, cumbersome containers. Many of the pickers, feeling the aches and pains of half a day's labor, stumbled through the dirt and rotting, crushed vegetables, hoisting their loads the best way they could—clasped two-handed across their bellies, slung over a shoulder, even straddled on a hip as they'd carry a child. Any way. The way that was easiest. Though there really was no easy way. Carrying the baskets was hard work no matter how it was handled.

Across the broad, unshaded field, as far as faces and crouched forms could be distinguished, there was the endless bobbing of heads and shoulders and the up-and-down, over-and-under, pistonlike pumping of arms and hands as the harvesters searched among the vines for the red fruit. In each row, ahead of each picker stood empty baskets waiting to be filled and carried to the end.

Some of the women and the young girls wore wide-brimmed hats, to provide whatever skimpy, sometimey shade a hat could afford under a relentless sun. A few had scarfs or kerchiefs around their heads, knotted at the base of their skulls. Almost to the last female they wore slacks, men's pants, or overalls. The pants and the overalls were almost like a uniform for the women. A short-skirted, bare-legged picker would have been ill-equipped indeed for hunkering through the tomato vines on her hands and knees, dragging or pushing a five-eighths bushel basket along with her. A few wore housedresses over their pants, perhaps from a subconscious need to affect some kind of feminine attire. The hemlines of dresses were fouled with the red Florida dirt and the stains of crushed tomatoes, and the wide-brimmed straw hats were sweat-stained, just like the men's headwear.

The men and the boys were attired in all manner of

gear: lightweight summer wear, slacks, shirts, overalls, blue denims. Anything.

The profane, belligerent, mid-fortyish man who worked a few rows away from mine, affected a baseball cap perched askew on the side of his head. The front of the cap bore the distinctive insignia of the New York Yankees baseball club. Perhaps he had worked somewhere near St. Petersburg to the north, where the Yankees once maintained spring training quarters. Or he might have purchased the cap at a wayside general merchandise store during his travels. Whatever the source, the belligerent one wore his cap with all the aplomb of a star centerfielder as he lugged his filled-up tomato baskets to row's end on one shoulder.

He carried a chip on the other shoulder.

"Hey, you, boy!" he shouted in my direction when he caught me scrutinizing him and making mental notes. "What the hell you lookin' at? You lost somethin' over here in this row? You work your own goddam row and never mind mine. I takes care of my business and it's up to you to take care of yours. I got enough trouble with the bossman all the time comin' round countin' my baskets 'thout you lookin' to see what I'm doin'. I ain't got no business in this goddam tomato patch nohow. This is the meanest way there is to make a livin', scroungin' aroun' here on my hands and knees and fillin' up these baskets to the top. Bossman is jus' evil enough not to pay me for them baskets I already picked. He done it before."

The centerfielder pointed angrily to his stacked baskets at the end of his row and whined, "He done it before, same bossman! Told the whole crew of us back there two, three weeks ago that the cannery had 'nough red ripes. Wasn't no use pickin' no more. An' that was after we'd been workin' from early mornin' till black dark, fillin' up these here baskets. . . . Yeah, I'm mad! I'm goin' stay mad long as I got to do this kind of work. Meanest way there is to make a livin'. You goddam right I'm mad and you ain't doin' me no good, standin' there payin' attention to what I'm doin'."

Another man in a row to my right, the stooped, sixtyish

one with the quiet mien and the air of detachment, wore a tattered Homburg as he bent to his labor. The hat had once been pearl gray, but now it was sweat-stained, weathered from exposure to many rainfalls and hot days under the sun and the dirt of many vegetable patches. I wondered if the once-splendid hat was a relic of an earlier, more prosperous era in his long life. Perhaps in better days he had worn it to church with appropriate pride, and with an appropriately well-pressed, double-breasted, blue serge department-store suit and a starched white shirt and a subdued polka-dot tie to set it off.

The elderly man moved very slowly, performing his work with a studied methodology. There was no wasted motion, no unnecessary effort. He appeared to concern himself not so much with the number of baskets he filled, or whether or not he kept abreast of the picker in the row alongside, but that his pace was steady and that no one interrupted him with small talk or complaints. He was a man of experience in gathering vegetables and he was aware of the limitations of his age. He knew that conversation interfered with his capacity to fill what few baskets he was capable of filling. Unlike the belligerent man with the baseball cap, he did not find it necessary to articulate his disdain for the work; only to approach it with the superb detachment that set him apart from the rest of the crew—an old man descending as effortlessly as he knew how down the slope of his declining years.

Red, at my left, was a tall man, well over six feet. His angular frame and jutting bones emphasized his height, so that he seemed to tower over his row. He was gaunt and emaciated. His light-colored skin, red-tinted and blotchy in spots, was drawn tightly over protruding elbows and knees, and over the high cheekbones of his face. His hair was short and uncombed. Tight little sand-colored curls, about the shade of the South Florida beaches, crawled out under his hatband, down both sides of his face, and along the back of his neck in two down-pointed arrows. It had been a long time since he'd visited the barber's. The thick lenses of the gold-rimmed spectacles he wore magnified his brown eyes. The heavy eyeglasses had the annoying habit of sliding down on the bridge of his nose in the sweat and grime. Regularly, almost automatically, he reanchored them with a forefinger. Sometimes he poked at them when it wasn't necessary, but it had become habitual, like blinking and squinting his eyes. When the spectacles slid out of place on the bridge of his nose, everything in his field of vision shifted out of focus. Consequently he inspected objects and people—and tomatoes—with a quizzical scowl which contorted his countenance.

Red's hands were completely out of proportion to the rest of his body. Their spread was enormous, like that of a great muscular Hercules. The fingers were long and well formed. The hands, probing among the vines, transferring tomatoes deftly, with machinelike precision to the baskets, were models of strength and power. They were hands that any artist would have been delighted to paint. Red's forearms were massive, too, and ample biceps bulged under his short-sleeved shirt. Yet his shoulders were narrow and angular like the rest of the body. The arms and hands seemed to belong to someone else. That's the kind of man Red was: he appeared to have been thrown together haphazardly, with little sense of proportion or form.

He coughed incessantly, and I shuddered each time I heard him. He doubled up, caught in an almost uncontrollable seizure. He growled and rumbled all the way down in his guts and brought up great gobs of mucus which he spat directionlessly into the burnt-orange Florida earth. I could see the red flecks in the miniature puddles of dirt and excrement. Sometimes, self-consciously, he kicked dirt over the spit and covered it up. He didn't always think to do it; or he perhaps didn't give a damn.

That was Red. He had active, galloping tuberculosis and he had known it for a long time before I performed an on-the-spot lay diagnosis.

He had it; he knew it; and there was nothing he could do to get rid of it. That was the way of a seasonal, migratory farm laborer. Life—such as it was under the searing Florida sun—had to go on for Red, or the harvesters stooped over in the rows would go on without him, pushing and shoving their baskets before them as they struggled to scratch from the earth their meager existence.

Red stretched his long frame to full height. He pulled the battered old straw hat from his head. His long fingers reached into a hip pocket and dragged out a dirty bandanna, the five-and-ten-cent store variety: a field of red stamped with black wagonwheels. He mopped the band of the ancient headgear and restored it to its proper place. At some time earlier, perhaps several seasons in the past, he had pocketknifed diamond-shaped holes in the crown to provide ventilation, but the top of it was blotted an indistinct gray-black by a mixture of perspiration and whatever dressing he used to control the tight little curls.

He unbuttoned his bleach-faded, bargain-counter sports shirt and dried carefully under his armpits. He unbuckled his pants, too, dropped them about butt high, and reached under his shirttail to wipe all around his waist. Before he pulled up his trousers he vigorously, unashamedly mopped the crotch between his legs. Having dried off everywhere he could reach he hitched the trousers back in place.

Then with a hooked finger he squeegeed the grime from his forehead. It didn't do much good. The oily, greenish-black bug spray encrusted his hands—as it did everyone's—and the venomous stuff had festered in the cuts and scratches he'd gotten searching through the vines. It discolored his khaki pants bottoms and covered his high-top army-surplus-store shoes. There was a dark film of the insecticide on the legs and on the seat of his pants where he had been wiping his hands.

Red half turned in my direction and observed over his shoulder, partly to me and partly to no one in particular:

"Been pickin' an' stoopin' an' grubbin' in dirt fields since I was a young un. Don't know nothin' else. Ain't never done nothin' else. My daddy did it before me; so did my ma." Red's declaration was delivered in the detached monotone which was characteristic of him. The tall fellow was hardly a talkative man. As a matter of fact, he was close-mouthed, tight-lipped. He rarely volunteered anything, though I had been bombarding him with leading, searching questions since just after dawn when we'd begun laboring under the warming sun at the head of adjoining rows. Now he squatted in the dirt, picked up a clod and slowly powdered it between a thumb and forefinger. The earth was a part of him. He had lived close to it for all of his life. There was a kinship between Red and the soil. He'd planted crops of all kinds, nurtured them, then gathered them up in baskets and boxes and hampers, and watched them hauled off to somewhere—on the way to somebody's larder. The powdered dirt trickled out of his fingers and he watched it intently, as though he thought his own life might be dribbling back to the dust whence it had come. And I noted once more the strength and dexterity of his hands.

Again he looked toward me, though not directly at me, and said, "You hustle an' tote and pick up these 'matoes from mornin' till night an' then the bossman don' wan' to pay you your wages. You be stoopin' over all day in the sun an' when the white man says he got him enough for the market, you done workin'. Ain't nothin' for you to do. Man, this is evilest kind of way to live. Can't hardly make a dime. Can't no more than stay alive. Me, I got all them chil'ren back there in that shack. They got to eat an' I got to work. My woman comes out here some days to pick, but she's got the miseries. Can't hol' things in her hands, specially when there's rain in the air. It's all she can do takin' care of them kids. Season's 'bout down now, here 'bouts, and we got to get on up the road. Needs money to pick up an' travel. Needs money to eat. Got to get someplace where the crops are. Like I said, don't know nothin' else."

Red was a seasonal farm worker. I had met him just after dawn that morning at the head of a long row of tomatoes in a field just outside Homestead, Florida—a busy, Dade County back-country village some thirty-five miles southwest of Miami. From Homestead and the surrounding villages and vegetable fields which line both sides of the country roads come the diming-room-table supplies for—well, everywhere.

I had arrived there in mid-April about the time the last wave of the early spring migrant tide was ebbing northward, "up the road, on the season." And I moved along with the migrant farm-labor army of stoop workers as they grubbed and lifted and sweated from the rich earth a large portion of the nation's—indeed, of the world's—harvest.

I got to know the tall, angular man with the big hands as well as one man can hope to know another in a few brief hot spring days. The story of his life, and that of his wife and small children, was one of misery and squalor; of hunger and hardship; of disinterest and despair; of days and weeks of hard labor under a punishing sun, for shamefully low wages. Indeed, the tragic chronicle of Red's forty-odd years of occupying so transiently each tiny successive fragment of somebody else's land, where he stood, or labored, or rested through all the dreary days of his life, appalled me, and I had thought myself rather well insulated against shock.

There were times in my all-too-short association with this particular harvester when I was aware of my intrusion into his life; my intimate, sometimes impertinent questions, were invasions of that privacy which ought to be sanctified, inviolate for every human being, not the least of all for Red. He had benefited so little from life; there was no reason to think, to dream, that his share of its rewards would ever be greater. Yet, there was within me the omnipresent urge—call it a mission if you like—to search out a particular kind of truth; a purpose which transcended the irreverence of trying to pry into another man's soul.

Red's brooding silence bespoke resentment. "What right have you," his puzzled brown eyes demanded, "to attempt to crawl into my skin, to ask about my woman and babies? You know nothing of who we are—or *why* we are what we are. You know nothing of our kind of suffering, or of our kind of fears.

"You don't belong here," his silence declared, "and who and what I am is none of your business."

But it was my business. It was, indeed, essential for me

to know about Red. He was the truth I sought, and his woman and babies were irrefutable confirmation of everything he said —or didn't say.

I visited with him and his woman and their brood of five barefoot, half-naked little children in the tin-and-tarpaper shanty that somebody else owned near Goulds, another Florida back-country farm village along the highway up the road on the way to Miami. And I found this migrant farm family carbon-copied with unhappy frequency many times over during the spring and summer and early fall of a long, close, painstaking look at the itinerant harvester along the Atlantic Seaboard. What I found in thousands of miles of travel, in many weeks of living and working and sleeping and, not infrequently, suffering with the gatherers of crops made me angry and sick. Just minutes away from the glittering, good-timing wealth of Miami Beach—and, later, just commuter-train distance away from the neon-lit vulgarity of Manhattan's Times Square—I saw the horrifying ugliness of poverty amid plenty. I saw Red and folks like him cheated out of their paltry wages for labor honestly done. I saw men and women and children crudely exploited by growers whose fields they harvested, and by migrant labor-crew leaders who brought them into those fields. I found that slavery had not been abolished. One hundred years after Abraham Lincoln had proclaimed emancipation in one of the great documents of our time there had not been deliverance. The American Promise remained woefully unfulfilled.

I rebelled at what I saw and experienced in the fields and farm-labor camps along the East Coast. I was shaken and grieved that the misery of marginal existence continued unrelieved in my lifetime. I was convinced that neither the declaration of War on Poverty—nor all of the other undeclared skirmishes—were likely to emancipate the itinerant gatherers of crops.

Red was one of the foot soldiers in that vast army, yet he was alone. The tall fellow's grave quietude suggested that he was a thoughtful man. He was at the same time a contradiction, displaying a recognizable intelligence, an inherent incisiveness in the face of almost total illiteracy.

"I don't remember," he said, "jus' how far I got in school. It weren't far, though—maybe a couple of grades or so, up in the Carolinas." He paused in mid-row, straddling the plants, hooked his thumbs in his waistband and pondered a moment. Then he observed: "Mus' be a whole lot of people in this country doin' the same kind of work as me. They ain't got no trade or nothin' an' so they got to do what they can. They can't be lawyers or preachers. They can't get out of the fields and into school to learn. So they jus' picks and totes and labors like this, till the bossman tells them to stop."

He unhooked his thumbs from his belt, and waved his hand over the field as he continued, "Maybe if I'd got a chance to stay in that school up in the Carolinas longer, I could have been the bossman of this here field. Then it would be me to tell folks when to start and when to stop and pay them off at the end of the day."

He kicked at an overripe tomato with his army-surplus-store shoes and squinted into the slanting rays of the sun. His spectacles slid down his nose and the rows and the people and the trees in the distance faded out of focus.

"Them children of mine . . . ," he said, pressing the glasses into place again with his forefinger, ". . . look like they got to come into these fields soon as they able, same as I did. Don't look much like they'll get any schoolin' no place. Sure like to see one of them boys be a preacher an' take the Word of the Lord aroun' to folks need religion. Needs a sight more of it myself. Ain't had time enough to stop long enough to git to the Good Book an' learn how to straighten myself out. Ain't no tellin'; one of them chil'ren maybe got enough sense to be a schoolteacher or somethin'. One of my kinfolk's a teacher in Georgia. That woman's got learnin'. She puts on a clean dress everyday and don' have no part of this pickin' an' liftin' on the road, on the season. That's the way to git by. Seems like my woman's all the time pregnant—or gittin' over it."

Twin girls had died early in infancy. They were buried, Red recollected, out back of a labor-camp shanty somewhere up the road—in one of the Carolinas. It was a source of the deepest regret to him that the course of his travels had not taken him back to the Carolina bean patches and the shanty where the babies had taken ill and died—of malnutrition and the lack of proper medical attention. Red lamented, "They passed away in the night from c'nsumption, long before they was old enough to know what it was all about. One went on Sunday, when we wasn't workin' in the fields; the other one died the next Wednesday—just like that. They was cryin' and squawlin' for their mother's breast one minute; then the next minute they was gone."

The lighting of a cigarette from a wrinkled, sweat-sodden packet did not interrupt Red's rare, fleeting moment of soul-baring. He continued: "The undertaker and the doctor said they got it from me. I been had it a long time. Ain' got no money for medicine or hospitals. Got all them chil'ren wants to eat. The old woman, she's porely, too, so I keeps on pickin' 'matoes—or whatever other kind of work they is to be done. Maybe this time, when the season is down, I'll git to a clinic someplace . . . maybe git me some pills. That's what I needs . . . some of them little pills and a bottle of cough syrup. That ought to stop this coughin' an' this pain in my chest. Sometimes I feels awful bad from the pain. Can't git my breath . . ."

He drew deeply from the cigarette, inhaled, coughed up a ragged cloud. "I hurts somethin' fierce here inside," he said. He crossed his arms tightly over the lower part of his chest. The misery that lived inside the tall man was painfully inscribed on his face. "Sometimes I hurts so bad," he said, "I can't hardly work in the fields. But there's them kids, an' my woman, Emily, she can't do nothin' to help. They all got to eat. Who's goin' to feed them . . . ?"

Thoughts of his family were more overpowering than the aches in his chest. "Emily's a good one," he said. "Works when she can. But she can't do much. Got too much misery in her joints. Can't tote a basket when she gits it filled up to the top. They tells me it's arthritis. Comes from sleepin' in a cold shanty one winter up in Virginia. Got stuck there after Christmas one year when she was havin' one of them kids."

There was George, he added, who was seven; and Marie, who was just four. They had developed coughs like his own ". . . back there two, three months ago, when it was cold at night in that shack in Goulds, an' there wasn't nothin' around to make no heat."

He wiped a bare forearm across his mouth and shrugged. "Maybe we'll all git to a clinic someplace and see 'bout some of them little pills. That ought to do it, them little pills.

". . . or maybe not."

Those were some of the grim facts of one migrant farm family's life: of the seven in the Alonzo Fisher family, four—Red himself, his wife, and two of the children—needed immediate, intensive medical care, considerably more than just little white pills from an outpatient clinic. Chances that they would get attention were, indeed, slim. The odds pointed, in fact, to quite the opposite: that Red's condition and that of his wife and children would deteriorate rapidly; that the other three still-unafflicted children might contract the rumbling cough that started down in his guts and came up in mucus flecked with blood.

Red ground the cigarette butt into the dirt with the heel of his shoe and having recovered, if only momentarily, from the coughing spell, he clamped his mouth shut. He was all finished stripping his soul to its nakedness. He pushed his magnifying-glass spectacles into place, rearranged his old straw and bent again to his labor. Squatting and crawling on hands and knees, pushing his basket before him, he was soon far down his row. Whatever other limitations ailments and worries had imposed upon the tall man, they had not yet inhibited his capacity for picking tomatoes. He worked with a rhythm and sureness acquired in crawling over many other long rows in other places—corn, or snap beans, or potatoes, or green peppers—harvesting anything there was to gather; toting whatever load there was to be lifted.

At the end of the row Red had stacked two or three times the number of baskets I had. There was no let-up in his smooth pace. Well, yes there was, too: he halted now and then to cough up mucus from deep down inside and spit it directionlessly into the dirt. But there were few other breaks in his rhythm.

The angular man with the protruding bones had not complained that hand-harvesting tomatoes is grueling, back-breaking, torturous work. It means stooping close to the earth from morning's half light until in the dusk it is no longer possible to distinguish the reds from the greens. It means lugging heavy baskets 150 to 200 feet to the end of the row after they are heaping full.

At row's end the contents of the baskets are checked for size and quality and ripeness. Then a crew of lifters and loaders stack them in the bed of a stake truck or trailer for shipment to market or the cannery or food-processing plant. The operation varies from field to field. Sometimes the pick is for unripe tomatoes for shipment to green-grocery wholesalers, where they ripen in bins or on shelves. But picking the greens involves the same wearying stoop-over-and-search, fill-up-the-basket kind of labor as the reds, though it is somewhat simpler. There is not the necessity for being selective as to the degree of ripeness. The greens are harvested for refrigerator-car shipment. The pinks are left on the vines to be harvested another day when they have become red ripe.

I had attempted to keep pace with Red Fisher only to ply him with questions. But now his discourse had been completed. There was no more for him to say. The brief periods he had spent talking with—rather, at—me had interfered with his labor and therefore lessened the amount he would earn. The few moments during which I had distracted Red had cost him money and there were, after all, all "them children to feed."

I sped up my own work only when the field boss happened into my area. A hulking, monstrous man, he weighed fully 300 pounds. He smoked a cigar and for reasons that only he was aware of he smoked it with the brand band still in place near the ragged end he clutched in his teeth. He wore knob-toed brown-and-white spectator shoes, run down at the heels and spotted with the omnipresent greenish-black bug spray. The field workers called him "Cowboy," and the reason was clear. He affected an egg-shell-white, broad-brimmed Texas-style ten-gallon hat. Unlike the worn-out, unkempt spectator shoes, the sombrero was spotlessly clean and carefully creased in the correct Southwestern manner. The hat, the cigar, and the incongruous shoes were Cowboy's marks of distinction and he wore them with self-conscious pride. They bestowed upon him—so he thought, anyway—the status he needed to elevate him several cuts above the common stoop laborers. It was obvious that he regarded himself as a person of substance, a man of position.

The manner in which Cowboy puffed his cigar spelled out his self-esteem. It was like a ritual. He billowed great bursts of the blue smoke with calculated gusto; then he contemplated the wispy clouds as they faded away in the breeze off the Keys. The inscription he wrote in smoke clouds in the heavy air above the long-rowed tomato patch was there for every last picker to read and take note of:

I AM SOMEBODY!
I AM THE BOSS!

Once, when I straightened up for a minute, Cowboy peered at me through a haze of cigar smoke and bellowed, "Bend your back, boy! You can't pick no tomatoes standin' there lookin' around." It was warning enough. I went back to picking tomatoes, filling the baskets, and lugging them to the end of the row.

To a gangly, middle-aged woman a few rows away Cowboy shouted, his voice menace-laden, "Git down there with it, woman! You come onto this field to pick them things up, not to yackety-yack to everybody around you. I wanna see all them there baskets filled up to the top. Git to hustlin' or you don' git no pay!"

The woman scowled and muttered profanities under her

breath. She was careful, though, that the big man didn't hear her, and she looked at him with utter contempt. She opened her mouth once to reply to the fat field boss, but then she reconsidered, and the words died in her throat. Maybe, she thought, I'd better not say nothing to that big bastard. I don't know what he might do. She clapped her floppy, beribboned straw hat on her head, readjusted the blue denims she wore under a housedress, and went back to her work. She wanted no trouble with the cigar smoker. Nobody else did, either.

The field where we worked near Homestead was rectangular. The rows of tomatoes, running lengthwise, stretched away almost to the horizon. Timber and brush had long ago been rolled off the flatlands and the rich burnt-orange of the earth had been carefully, precisely stitched in parallel rows. It was as though the tractor driver at plowing time had been guided along a geometric course by a compass, never diverting except at the end of each row where he had wheeled his machine around to follow the same pattern in reverse. About half the field workers picked from one end of the field and the others worked from the other. Some ingenious field boss (not the fat cigar smoker, I am certain) had discovered that competition between and among humans is instinctive and that efficient production of hand harvesters increases when they work toward each other from opposite ends of the same row.

Columns of tall pines surrounded the field on all four sides. At the most distant end, somewhere beyond the pines, a noisy tractor, its engine missing and backfiring now and then, was turning picked-out tomato vines back into the earth for the next crop—possibly corn. You could hear the erratic throb of the engine as it made its way up and down the field.

Three or four old rattletrap buses were drawn up in the shade of a platoon of maples at one end of the field. They bore South Carolina and Florida license plates and they appeared to have been resurrected from one or another of the weed-grown vehicle graveyards which lie just outside almost every Southern town. It was a sorry collection of wrecks and the only resemblance the buses bore to each other was that they were all in a state of disrepair. Some were a little shabbier, more in need of paint and patching, than others, but they all seemed to be in a state of advanced senility—or to have been damaged by head-on collisions with others of their kind. This was the transportation, such as it was, that the crew leaders used to freight their human cargoes of field laborers back and forth between farm towns, or farm-labor camps, and the acreage to be harvested. Across the sidepanels of one of the buses someone with only minuscule knowledge of the sign-painting craft had daubed these words:

COWBOY'S ARK
Farm Labor for Hire
Perrine, Fla.

There was no mistaking that this particular vehicle was the property of the fat crew boss. At least outwardly its condition was better than the rest of the fleet. For this day's voyage, it was the flagship, and it was commanded by a Texas-style admiral whose emblems of authority were the big cigar, the spectator shoes, and the ten-gallon hat.

A half-dozen men lounged in and around the buses. Some sat in the drivers' seats. Others sprawled and snored fitfully in the meager shade of the maples—or they smoked cigarettes and told lies about the women they'd laid. They didn't have to lie about the money they'd made at the expense of the sweating, stooped-over field hands who labored up and down the rows. They had made money, a considerable amount of it. That was part of the curious caste system within which farm-labor crews work. It is the role of the leader to recruit and transport the hand harvesters, but not to perform stoop-over work in the fields like the hired hands. It is the leader's function to hire workers as cheaply as he can and deliver them wherever they are needed. Then, at the end of the day, it is his job to return the field hands to wherever he found them—a farm-labor camp in Goulds or Perrine; a street corner in Miami or Jacksonville; wherever a farm hand could be located who was ready and willing and able to bend over all day in the heat and gather the crops. The crew leader's fee was computed by the number of workers he brought into a field and the number of baskets, hampers, or burlap bags they filled—and the unit pay rate that prevailed for the day.

Cheating in all of its crudity was inherent in the complexities of the pay rate for "day-haul" labor. The grower cheated the field boss; the field boss cheated the crew leader, and it was inevitable that the field hand, the man—or woman or child—at the bottom of the ladder, was cheated by everyone else. He was least able to defend himself against fraud and therefore most susceptible to exploitation. It was the stoop laborer's lot to struggle and fight and scrape for the little bit left after the others got theirs.

I learned early via the tomato-row grapevine how one of the basic frauds operates: A field boss contracts with a grower to harvest a specified number of acres for a given amount of money. Because he is a field boss, he is generally knowledgeable enough to have calculated how much labor the job will require and how long it will take to get the crops in. Through informal, oral agreements, he subcontracts the work to the necessary number of crew leaders. They also have special talents: they know how and where to recruit field hands, how to transport them to fields at minimum cost, and how to extract the maximum amount of work from them for the least pay. Where a building contractor commonly performs work on a cost-plus basis, the farm-labor crew boss fulfills his contract through a less-than-cost scheme. He inflates his price to the field boss or grower who hires the field hands he provides, then operates on a maximum-profit margin, with labor getting the short end.

Corruption is built into the system all the way along the line. The grower contracts with field bosses for the skimpiest price. The field boss assures himself a good middleman profit by making sinister, clandestine deals with his crew leaders. The crew leader cheats on both ends of his deal—with the field boss and with the hired hands. It becomes inescapable that stoop laborers find their days' wages shaved to the bone by the profiteers on levels above. In many instances there is no middleman between the crew leader and the grower. The contract—more often verbal than written—is made directly between the producer who has crops to be gathered and the crew boss who can deliver the hands to get the work done. No matter what the variety of the fraud practiced, the man or woman, boy or girl, whose muscle and sweat fill the baskets get the short end of the deal. Checks and safeguards against cheating in the migrant-farm-labor stream are, in most instances, negligible. They have virtually no effect.

It was my misfortune—and Red's—to be assigned to rows facing westward. As the sun arched its way into midafternoon, its rays shone directly into our eyes when we stood to stretch or to carry our baskets to the end of the line. A rural entrepreneur had driven a mobile lunch wagon between the rows and located it in the center of the broad field so that it was accessible from all directions. Two homely, teen-age girls, probably the lunch-wagon man's daughters, dispensed greasy, tough-skinned pork-sausage sandwiches for 35 cents each. And, if you were hardy, or thirsty enough, you could purchase strawberry soda pop (imitation flavor added, it said on the labels) for 20 cents. The soft drinks were tepid, the ice in a laundry-tub container having melted well before noon in the heat. Not far from the lunch wagon the men who worked for the field boss had installed a 100-gallon wooden barrel and equipped it with a sawed-off-at-the-top pineapple-juice can. The label read: "Libby's—A Superior Product." This held the drinking-water supply for the crew of 200-odd field workers, assorted checkers, loaders, and truck drivers. It was a community watering place in every sense of the word and no signs said "Colored" or "White," though there were in the fields a scattered few white men working in supervisory positions. Those who had not brought their own personal drinking containers—and very few had—shared the pineapple-juice can and sanitation was a word that not many knew anything about.

After you filled your basket with red ripes you lugged it to the end of the row the best way you could. There, a checker inspected it to make sure the tomatoes were of the right size and ripeness. The checker sometimes spot-checked a basket or two in each end-of-the-row stack to satisfy himself that there were no greens or rotted vegetables under the top layer. Once a watery-eyed man with a cud of snuff under his lower lip stopped at the end of my row, jammed his arm up to the elbow into a basket and warned, "Don't let me ketch you cheatin'! If I finds any greens or rottens in here anyplace, I'll dump the whole goddam basket out on the ground. That'll learn ya. These here 'matoes is goin' to the cannery and bossman don' want no green ones mixed up."

I had no doubt that Watery Eyes would make good his threat. I had watched him dump into the dirt between the rows several baskets belonging to the belligerent man with the baseball cap. Watery Eyes, however, had to justify his position as a checker. He had earned a promotion from stoop laborer and was now being paid a dollar an hour. If he didn't do what the bossman told him to do, he'd be rapidly, unceremoniously demoted back to stooping and crawling along on his hands and knees like Red and myself. When the checker dumped a basket out on the ground it canceled out 15 to 20 minutes of the profane centerfielder's labor. It made him boiling mad.

Yet cheating was part of the game. It was expected. I had learned from other pickers early in the day how to fill three-quarters of my baskets with greens or rottens, then cover the top over with red ripes. "Don't make too much difference," Red told me, "when they git to the cannin' plant. Don't nobody know who picked them an' they all goes into a bin and gits mixed up with the ripe ones and the bugs. If they ketch ya," he cautioned, "you lose the time it took to fill up the basket; and then that checker man keeps bloodshot eyes on your stack."

If the checker approved your filled-up, stacked baskets, he gave you a ticket for each of them, much like the one the box-office girl grinds out of a dispensing machine at the movies. Watery Eyes counted carefully and tore the tickets from a long roll which he carried tied to his belt by a string. His was the easiest job in the fields and there was a certain amount of responsibility attached to it. Who would have known the difference had he made a deal with a friend to dispense two tickets, instead of one, for each basket picked, and split the graft down the middle? The checker assigned to my row hardly conveyed an image of trust and honor. I was certain that he had made deals with perhaps a half-dozen friends and was sharing the gravy 60 per cent for himself and 40 per cent for each co-conspirator. He walked leisurely from one row-end to another, inspecting the harvest for quality and size, all the time picking his teeth with a wood matchstick. The rate that day was 12 cents per basket. A week ago it had been 15 cents, but as the crops matured and the season progressed, the market price had dropped. There was a surplus of tomatoes at the cannery and at the wholesale buyers'. Brokers, dealers, and wholesalers had, in the inevitable course of the law of supply and demand, tailored their prices to fit the market, and the stoop laborer was the first to feel the pinch.

By the time the late afternoon sun slanted over the pine trees at the far end of the field I had collected 36 of the tickets which Watery Eyes had torn from the roll tied to his belt. I had also collected a thick crust of oily insecticide on my hands and arms all the way up above my elbows. A rapid mental calculation told me the 36 tickets would add up to $4.32—my reward for ten hours of bending and picking, of searching through the vines for the red ripes. Those ten hours had taken their toll. The muscles along the backs of my legs, across the small of my back and up into my shoulders and upper arms ached murderously. I hurt everywhere. My pants legs were ragged and stained with insect spray from crawling along on my hands and knees through the rows. Blood had scabbed over the many abrasions I'd acquired on my legs and hands in encounters with rocks. I limped slowly, wearily, haltingly to the end of the row to make a final count of the stack. There was no mistake; I could account for only 36 baskets. Another stoop-shouldered field laborer was there, too, making his count. In his ten hours of work, pushing and shoving his baskets before him the same way I had, he had collected only 27 tickets. They would earn him only $3.24.

"You takes what the bossman gives you," he said. "Ain't nothing else you can do, is there?" He hunched his shoulders in a shrug, spread his hands in a palms-down, what-can-you-do-about-it gesture and declared: "You jus' gits them tickets when the man comes around an' that's the bes' you can do. You turns them in at the end of the day and you takes what the bossman hands you in your hand. When the field is picked clean here and there ain' nothin' else lef' to do, you moves on somewhere else, up the road."

He scooped up a handful of the Florida dirt and rubbed it briskly along the backs and sides of his arms and hands; it did remove some of the bug spray—a little, not much. This was another trick you learned in the fields. There are techniques in this business as in every other. My performance compared to Red's and that of most of the others showed that I had not acquired much finesse. In the actual picking, for instance, the trick is to grasp the vegetable with the palm of the hand, as you would a doorknob, then snap it off with a finger tip at the stem. After a time you learn to do it almost by instinct, with the sureness of touch which marks you, like Red, as a field laborer of experience.

When the white bossman set up his pay station in the back of his new Dodge pickup truck, nearly 200 field hands lined up for their day's wages. The line moved rather quickly, for the bossman didn't have to pay out very much. He had equipped the pay station with a table which told him exactly how much cash to pay out in exchange for any given number of tickets. He had a stack of crisp, new $1 and $5 bills and a tomato carton filled with rolled coins. When my turn came, he handed me four new one-dollar bills, two dimes, two nickels and two pennies—$4.32.

By that time the few clouds that had blown in from the southeast on the winds off the Keys were gold-edged in the declining sun. The breeze had freshened a bit and there was in the air a smell of lush, rich, growing things—the pines surrounding the fields, a stand of wild aromatic vegetation somewhere, a faint suggestion of the salt-sea Atlantic not too far distant.

It was the end of a punishing day, perhaps the most strength-sapping labor I had ever done. It took all the reserve I could muster just to wait in the line, then shuffle up to the bossman for my pay. Red was a few yards ahead of me and, by the time I had collected my little handful of change, he had already boarded Cowboy's bus for the trip home. When I sat down beside him, I found that he was ready to unburden himself of a few more thoughts, this time without my prodding. Though the weariness in my muscles and joints, the aches across my shoulders and back made conversation a real chore, I would not have lost a rare opportunity to share the thoughts of the slender, quiet man who thought more of his family than of the persistent cough that wracked his insides.

"You been worryin' me about the woman an' kids," he announced, "so I'm goin' to take you to see 'em. It ain't far from here, 'bout nine or ten miles up the way on the main highway. When you gits ready to leave, you can walk out to the road and ketch you a bus to Miami. Don't cost but a quarter or thirty-five cents. Ain't no space for you to stay for the night in that little shanty. Cowboy lets a whole gang of us off up at Goulds, an' he picks us up again in the morning."

By stretching imagination to the limit one might describe the place where Alonzo Fisher lived with his wife, Emily, and their five children as a single-dwelling unit in a suburban housing development. It qualified in one respect: it was just a dozen or so miles from Miami, within easy commuting distance. It sat in the midst of a cluster of similar residences on a two-acre plot of land a few hundred yards west of U. S. Highway No. 1. Scattered irregularly around the Fisher abode were ten or twelve one- and two-room shanties, all occupied, all of them of like construction. The shacks were in pretty much the same condition as Red's, which is to say that they appeared in imminent danger of collapsing into ten or twelve piles of debris. None were more than just barely habitable; their sameness also might have qualified them as part of a development, but that was as far as the projection could legitimately extend. Perhaps they had been constructed sometime in the distant past by the same builder. Or maybe they had been erected by different persons using the same plan, or no plan at all.

I arrived there with Red after a short walk from the roadside stop where Cowboy had paused briefly to let us hop off his crowded bus. We were at the tail end of a hard day's labor and the exertion had done nothing to improve the tall fellow's health. He was caught up in another coughing attack as he led me down a dirt road into a stand of pine trees. The development, nestled in a small V-shaped hollow, was shielded from view by a thick growth of wild underbrush. For anyone who didn't know the precise direction, the place would have been almost impossible to find. There was no name for the dirt pathway that led to the cluster of shanties; there was no number over Red's door, nor over the doors of his neighbors. His shack just stood there, unashamedly, the middle one in a row of three. A hill covered with waist-high foliage sloped away to the rear of the plot. You approached the Fisher place by picking your way, stumbling a little, down a small incline which was one side of the V. Beyond the crest of the other side there was a large warehouse-like building with piles of rusted road-construction machinery and bits and pieces of indistinguishable vehicles leaning against its walls. There was an air of decay and abandonment around the building, as if the owners had gone away four or five years ago with the intention of coming back and had later changed their minds. Weeds and grass had sprung up around a wheelbarrow propped against the warehouse door.

To the right of Red's shanty was a similar, though smaller, one. Its roof was of corrugated metal, perhaps zinc; its siding of red simulated-brick shingling. A hardware-store lock and a clasp anchored with carpenter's nails fastened the front door from the outside. A large washtub hung from a nail beside the door. Red's next-door neighbors, whoever they were, seemed not to be at home.

The door to the place on the left hung slightly ajar.

Through it I could see a man, attired only in loafer-type oxfords and underwear, eating his evening meal. There was a loaf of grocery-store bread on the table, a stove-blackened coffeepot nearby and from a large plate the man scooped with considerable relish some manner of migrant-farm-laborer's fare. A huge black dog slumbered beneath the table, ignoring the clanking of silverware as the man busily shoveled whatever it was into his mouth in great spoonfuls, seemingly unaware of the two of us stumbling down the slope in the half-light of dusk.

From the pair of four-by-four timbers that supported the tiny porch in front of the Alonzo Fisher place hung a clothesline. From it, one quickly concluded that the family was predominantly female: rayon slips and panties of various sizes, an oversize brassiere, a half-dozen dishcloths and a bath towel or two. There was a single pair of men's work pants, and it was easy to see that they belonged to a stoop worker. They were worn thin at the knees and along the thighs there was the dark, telltale stain of the bug spray that neither scrub board nor washing machine would ever get out. Here, too, a washtub hung from a nail beside the door, and draped over the low rickety railing around the porch were a little girl's anklets and a pair of blue sneakers with white rubber soles, washed and set out to dry for wear the next day.

Four sets of cinder blocks supported the wood-frame shingled shanty at each of its four corners, elevating it perhaps two or two and one-half feet off the ground. Two additional stacks of cinder blocks somewhat precariously held up the tiny front porch. The uniformity of construction, so characteristic of housing developments, whether town or suburban, whether by accident or design, was just as evident in the back-country Dade County community where Alonzo Fisher lived with his family. Like all of its neighbors, this development was weather-worn and wind-beaten.

"Come on in," Red invited. "This place ain't nothin' special, but you said you wanted to meet the woman and them there chil'ren, an' see how we live. Ain't nothin' much to look at, but you're welcome to see. Been here 'bout two months now, since when the crops started to come in good. Season's 'mos down in this part of the country and we'll be gittin' on up the road, somewhere else."

Red's lumber-yard-brick castle measured some ten feet and a few odd inches across and twelve to fourteen feet from the threshold of the front door to the back wall. A kerosene lantern, its wick turned low to conserve fuel and minimize smoke, cast dim, flickering shadows on the walls. A blanket, hung from a clothesline, stretched across the right side of the room, dividing it into two compartments. The blanket hung to a point just short of the floor and behind it I could distinguish children's shoes and sneakers and socks and clothing under a bed.

Emily Fisher arose from her seat at the kitchen table. She was an ample woman, as striking for her girth and large bosom as her husband was for his elongated thinness. She got up slowly, leaning her full weight on the table for support, and grasping the back of a chair to pull herself erect. She was shy, reticent, even more withdrawn than her husband; the mere act of nodding her head in acknowledgment of his introduction was obviously a difficult task. I did not add to her discomfort by probing questions such as I had been putting to Red during the day.

"How ya do?" she mumbled and slid back into her chair by the table with noticeable effort, again grasping the chair back for support and resting one hand on the table. There were the remains of the evening meal: a plate of fried chicken, a pan of cornbread, a few boiled potatoes, and a green leafy vegetable.

To the left of the entrance door, immediately inside, stood a two-burner kerosene stove, a coffeepot on one burner, a frying pan on the other, its bottom covered with a film of the grease in which Emily Fisher had cooked the chicken. There was a sink next to the stove, but there were no faucets for running water. The back of the sink was mounted in some way on the wall. The two front corners were supported by wood posts which were nailed to the floor. Though a drainpipe led from the drain hole in the back of the sink through the wall to the outside, I could not find at first glance any source of water supply. Red cleared that point up when he saw me inspecting the sanitary facilities. He reached under the sink, felt around for a moment, and drew out a bucket of water. The bucket was the kind housewives generally use for scrubbing, but he dipped water from it, poured it into a glass and handed it to me. It was for drinking.

"You want some?" he inquired.

I declined with profuse thanks. The memory of the tall fellow's frequent unrelieved seizures were to remain forever etched in my mind. And there was the thought that two of his young children had the same kind of rumbling cough. . . .

A three-quarter-size mattress on a steel frame occupied most of the space along the back wall. There was a chair at the head of the bed and a slop jar, for late night toileting, at the other end. The bed was covered with a rough, off-white muslin sheet tucked and folded neatly at each corner, hospital style. A heavy olive-drab blanket was folded across the foot of the bed, but there were no pillows. There was a window in the center of the back wall directly over the bed, but a wrinkled green blind had been thumbtacked over it, so that there was no view from the rear of the Fisher shack. Another window above the kerosene stove looked out over the shanty next door, the one occupied by the man we had seen eating his dinner in his undershirt.

"The kids is asleep, all of 'em," Red declared as he draped his long frame over a chair. "You c'n see 'em if you want to, but they's all asleep. Don't wake 'em up! Look behind that blanket hangin' up an' that's where they are."

I had so much wanted to see and talk to them. I wanted to know some of the facts of a migrant-farm-worker's life through the eyes of his children, but I was reluctant to disturb their slumber. I pulled back a corner of the divider blanket and the errant rays of the kerosene lantern threw tiny fingers of light into the gloom. The three youngest children lay sleeping crosswise on one bed. It was a sagging, mesh-spring piece of antiquity and the small forms were spread-eagled wherever they could find space. The stale odor of damp, moldy cotton was mixed with the moist tang of human perspiration in the tiny space. Two other children slept close together on a narrow cot next to the larger bed. From somewhere in the dark corner nearest the right wall came the heavy, labored breathing of one of the children, gasping, fighting to fill his lungs with more air. Springs creaked as one of the tiny forms shifted in a subconscious search for more space.

A feeling of nausea crept up from my stomach into my throat and I dropped the corner of the blanket back into place. There in the darkness of that broken-down red-shingled shack, I saw and smelled and heard the hopelessness, the futility, of one migrant-farm-worker's family. I knew the sickness that lived in one man's chest, the same agony that—along with inadequate and improper food—had already sent two of his little ones to their graves.

"Toilet's out in the back," Mrs. Fisher volunteered, perhaps detecting a look of illness on my face. "Whole lots of folks use it," she added, "so if it's busy, you go out in the woods. When we can't wait, we goes out 'hind a tree." This was a rare burst of volubility for Red's woman, but she warmed up even more: "Maybe twenty-five or thirty people uses that toilet, 'cluding a lot of kids. Most times we can tell when it's busy, 'cause the door squeaks one way when you goes in and another way when you comes out. Ain't heard no squeakin' noises in a spell, so I guess you can go if you want to."

I was anxious to get out of the heavy, foul air of Mr. and Mrs. Alonzo Fisher's shanty, but I was there as an invited guest and there simply was no escape, not for a while.

So we talked for half an hour or so and I learned that they rented the place from a landlord named Mr. Clay, but they saw him, or one of his numerous sons or agents, only on Saturday morning when the rent was due. There was no heat in any of the dwellings, with the exception of the kerosene cookstove; and there was no light except for the kerosene lanterns that each family had purchased down the road at the general merchandise store which Mr. Clay and his sons ran.

It was the lot of Alonzo (Red) Fisher to live and sleep

and eat—and suffer—with his woman and his five children in this back-country Dade County suburban housing development, along with ten or twelve neighbor migrant-farm-labor families. They shared these mean quarters with an assortment of vermin, insects, and other crawling, slithering things, the true census of which no one knew. It was a pitiable environment, pregnant with all of the elements conducive to disease and early fatality; the kind of evil atmosphere in which the Fisher young ones suffered and strained for breath in their moldy, creaking mesh-spring bed behind the hanging blanket. It was marginal living in all of its shocking crudity, a dozen or so miles from plush Miami.

Alonzo and Emily Fisher's children had been conceived, born, and reared in a succession of such migrant-farm-labor settlements. So, for that matter, had Red and his wife. Demanded from them for their existence on this tiny portion of Mr. Clay's land was $13.50 every Saturday morning when one of the sons or the agents came by. It was just enough space to be born in; it was at the same time enough to lay down and die in.

Red and Emily Fisher were hunched over their dinner table in the gloom of the flickering kerosene lamp when I left, and the children were tossing fitfully in the compartment behind the blanket.

Red's directions were precise. I stumbled back up the incline to the pathway and followed it to U. S. Highway No. 1, a hundred yards or so to the east. After a short wait, a commuter bus did indeed screech to a halt at the side of the highway and I climbed aboard for the trip to Miami, the thought of sleep in a hotel bed between sheets uppermost in my mind. I was too weary to eat anything, and too preoccupied by my encounter with the seven Fishers even to consider doing *anything* else.

2

Up the Road to Nowhere

I caught the same bus back to Homestead early the next day where, in the first light of the morning sun, farm-labor crew leaders were already at work rounding up hands. Rudy Thompson had driven his ancient converted school bus into a debris-littered vacant lot in the middle of "colored town" and was hard at work with his sales pitch. "Come on here," he shouted to anyone who would listen. "I got work for anybody who wants to make money. Goin' up the road soon's this bus is loaded. There's tomatoes and snap beans fallin' off the vines where I'm goin' and there's so much cabbage to chop you can't see to the end of the field. Come on here, everybody!"

A few men and boys, some of the latter in their early

'teens, clustered around the waving, bellowing crew leader. He stood on an empty milk crate so that he could have a better view of the crowd scattered around the lot and so that each of these potential farm laborers could have a better view of him.

The dusty little farm town was overrun with idle field hands, even at that hour between dawn and the brightness of day. There was little work for them in the surrounding fields, so they loafed in and around the tavern, or in the grocery store next door. They leaned against unpainted, one-story pine-board buildings along the dirt street, drinking strawberry soda pop to kill time, or smoking cigarettes while they waited for something to happen. They would just wait, hope, and hang around until some kind of gainful employment presented itself. Then they'd be off to wherever the crops were.

Most of them had worked only part time—a day or two, a few hours—during the end-of-the-season weeks; then the tractors had come along, dragging the big plow assemblies behind them, turning the picked-out tomato vines back into the earth for the next planting.

That was the way it was in a farm town: the harvest was in and suddenly, almost overnight, there was an oversupply of labor, and an undersupply of funds. The men and boys, and a few women, were anxious for something to do. They jingled around in their pockets the few coins they had left—enough for a soft drink or two and an occasional pack of cigarettes. Sometimes there was enough cash for a bottle of 49-cents-a-quart wine from the grocery store—that is if two or three purchased it jointly. But in that case there was almost always an argument about someone drinking more than his share.

"How much you payin' for 'matoes?" one man inquired of the crew leader. "Is it by the day or at the end of the week, or when?"

"It's fifteen cents for a basket," Rudy informed him, "and I pay every man every day. It's all clean work; no broken-down shanties to live in and everybody gets blankets and sheets. The farmer don't charge nobody no rent to live there. You start workin' and makin' money the minute we get there an' every bit of it's yours. There's plenty of work to do an' there ain't nothing taken out of your pay."

Robert Andrew Robinson edged his way closer to the sweating, fast-talking crew leader. He listened awhile, scratching his head. Then he made up his mind to speak. "You carryin' families with kids?" he asked. "Is there someplace we can stay together, me and my old lady and the kids?"

Rudy's glibness was as polished as that of a carnival pitchman. He leaned down from the milk-crate platform, placed a friendly, reassuring arm on Robert's shoulder and affirmed, "We don't bar nobody. We're takin' every man, woman, and child that wants to work. Just you and your old lady get on this bus. We'll be ready to leave here just as soon as we get it filled up."

That was guarantee enough for Robert. "Wait here!" he said. "Don' go no place without me! I got to git 'em all together and ready to leave."

With one family—at least two pickers—recruited, Rudy went again into his loud, exaggerated assurances of Utopia up the road. They had a familiar ring. I had heard his story, and a good many variations, before—on a street corner in Miami, in a parking lot in Perrine, at a beer-and-wine tavern in Goulds—wherever out-of-work farm hands gathered, wherever crew bosses trafficked in human misery by the busload. Rudy's promises of a land of milk and honey up the road, his assurances that a harvest of dollar bills was ripe for the picking were a chronicle of deception refined to an exact science by many unscrupulous crew bosses. The tools of their trade are promises. The harvest up the road is often one of drudgery and despair.

In a few minutes Robert Andrew Robinson had rounded up his family with all of their earthly possessions and was ready to move. He herded them out of the tar-paper shack that leaned for support against an old barn on a side lot. He carried a bedspread tied by its four corners and containing one half of the family's belongings. On his shoulder in a cardboard carton (Pabst's Blue Ribbon—The Original Milwaukee Beer) was the rest of the Robinson family's material wealth.

With his dark, rail-thin wife trailing obediently behind him, cradling their infant son, Robert installed the beer-carton suitcase and the bedspread laundry bag in a seat near the front of Rudy Thompson's rattletrap. Behind that he made a place for himself, his wife Mattie, and fat little sleeping Adolphus.

Seven-year-old Virginia Lee came along a little later, clutching a rubber doll in one hand, a picture book in the other. As she hop-skipped up the two steps into Rudy's aging crew bus to join her migrating family she asked, "Momma, will there be a school where we're going? There wasn't none at the last place and there ain't no schoolhouse here. You said before we'd be someplace where there's a school to go to. Will there be one up the road?" The little girl settled into the seat her daddy had assigned to her and looked expectantly at her mother. "Will that schoolhouse be here, like you said? Huh?"

The woman shifted the infant in her arms, then looked at her husband, who pretended not to have heard. To avoid answering the question Mrs. Robinson busied herself with the baby. She felt under the rubberized pants to see if his diaper was wet. She picked his nose with her little finger, then wiped it across her breasts. She looked out at the haranguing crew boss, still telling his story from the milk crate in the vacant lot. Finally, she darted a quick look at Virginia Lee and said wearily, "We'll see honey. We'll see."

That was all. There was nothing more.

Weariness and despair—perhaps more than anything else, defeat—were clear in Mattie Robinson's voice and written across her care-worn face. Virginia Lee sensed the hopelessness, too, as she waited, wide-eyed, for something more from her mother. But there was nothing more she could say. She hadn't the courage to expand on the answer. She knew the danger of making promises to the child. She knew that Virginia Lee would not forget. It was easier not to make promises that one day she might not be able to keep.

Through the day I walked about the farm village from one end to the other in search of a farm-labor-crew to join. A few crews were bound for Carolina sweet corn, then on to early Virginia and Maryland strawberries. Others were making ready for the long trip to Delaware, for the potato crop when it was ready, and during the interim there might be a few weeks of asparagus and green peppers. Some of the crews were bound for New Jersey and upstate New York. A bus or two was loading for the long trip to New York's upper Hudson Valley apple and peach orchards, then perhaps to turn southward again by way of Long Island and southern New Jersey. Still other crews might branch off to the west, toward Pennsylvania and Ohio for turnips and green peppers. There was an established pattern in the migrant flow, but there were many tributaries leading off from the main stream.

For my purposes long hauls to Pennsylvania or northern New York would have consumed far too much time. I wanted to learn more of the farm workers at the fountainhead of the migrant stream—as they finished their labors in one field and moved along slowly, crop by crop, to the next. I decided that Rudy Thompson's crew was ideal. It was a representative cross section of varied ages, both men and women. None had earned—or been able to save—anything to amount to much for several weeks. All were literally without funds. The crew included the Robinson family of four; a paunchy, tight-trousered effeminate man of about thirty who all but wept openly at the prospect of leaving his mother behind; and a nondescript group of rough male field hands. There was one other married couple in the crew of seventeen. I had overheard the two of them plotting a sinister conspiracy against Rudy Thompson as they climbed into his bus. They would get a free ride as far north as Rudy carried them. Then, at their first chance, they would desert the crew and hitch other rides going farther up the road. Apparently they had kinfolk in Philadelphia, and the woman was determined to get to the big city the best way she could. Silently, I wished them success in their plot. My sympathies rested with any one of the crew who had even the most remote chance to escape it.

Almost without exception the men carried all of their belongings in bundles under their arms. A few had brown-paper grocery-store shopping bags crammed to the top with shirts, underwear, and extra pants. One or two of them had their possessions rope bound in cardboard canned-goods cartons. They were just as easy to manage as a valise if you knew how to tie a handle into the rope.

One conspicuous nonconformist carried a battered suitcase. They called this middle-aged man W.T., and he seemed a bit out of place in the ragtag band of harvesters. For one thing he wore a necktie with his multi-hued sports shirt. It didn't seem to matter to him that the green, white and black-checked short-sleeved shirt was completely out of harmony with the beige tie. And it apparently hadn't occurred to him that both belt and suspenders weren't necessary to support his tan work pants. Well, perhaps both were essential. I had no way of knowing the degree of dependability of either means of support; nor did I have any idea of the weight of the additional equipment he carried in his pockets—perhaps a razor on one side and a bar of soap or two on the other. He might even have had a fat wallet filled with laundry tickets, identification cards, and maybe a picture or two of folks he left behind somewhere. What *was* important to W.T.—and this was clearly discernible in the square-set, firmly anchored position of his felt hat—was the fact that he was costumed for travel in the best that he owned. Whoever didn't approve of it could go to hell.

By the time Rudy had assembled his crew (the seventeen were all he could muster) and maneuvered his bus out of the vacant lot in Homestead, careening around curves and up grades toward the highway, it was late afternoon. Every nut, every bolt, every inch of the vehicle trembled. The only distinction between his bus and a total wreck was the fact that it ran—rather fast, too; too damned fast to be safe. The name, CHEVROLET, was emblazoned across its grill. Perhaps fifteen or more years in the past, this bus had rolled off the General Motors assembly line in Detroit smelling of lubricating oil and fresh paint. The bus, now well into its declining years, was bent and misshapen. It had been repainted many times over in futile attempts to recapture the gloss and polish of its youth. The efforts had fallen short of the mark. One of its headlights had been battered askew, very likely in some losing engagement with the rear end of a truck. One front fender dangled weakly from its mounting, the result no doubt of an equally unfortunate clash with a telephone pole or a lamppost. Yet hand-splashed in bold black letters across the panels on both sides was this proud legend:

RUDOLPH T. THOMPSON
Farm Labor for Hire—By the Day or Season
ST. PETE, FLA.

Gaining entry to the creaking conveyance was a task in itself. The open-close lever, linked by a long metal arm to a ceiling-to-floor vertical column near the driver's seat, was inoperative. Years ago when GM had certified the bus as mechanically safe and ready to transport school children, the open-close device had operated in such a way that the driver could provide easy entry and exit by maneuvering a simple push-and-pull handle. This was no longer possible. Instead it was necessary to pry open one or the other of its two accordion doors by applying weight and force.

Inside chaos prevailed. The double seat immediately to the left of the entrance was backless; its stuffing and simulated leather covering had long since disappeared. Assorted boxes and bags occupied that space where the seat had once been. The Robinson family occupied two seats directly behind the driver's and the other crew members were scattered irregularly three-fourths of the way to the rear.

The back seats were stacked almost ceiling high with equipment: farm tools, repair gear for the bus, a spare tire or two, and boxes and baggage containing miscellaneous junk. A fifty-five gallon metal oil drum, the kind I had seen often in fields where the harvesters worked, was lodged firmly against the rear door. The words, "Emergency Exit," were still legible in red paint above it, but the latch and handle which had once promised escape in the event of accident were corroded and broken. Heavy-gauge baling wire bound the door tightly to the frame, but it rattled and creaked at every bump in the road.

Scattered along the aisle were the personal effects of the traveling harvesters: W.T.'s battered suitcase tied up with clothesline, shopping bags and cartons belonging to the less affluent travelers. Near the front the Robinson family's bedspread bundle of laundry blocked the way. Except for the front door, access to which was barred by the legs and bodies and baggage of the crew Rudy had gathered, there was absolutely no way out. . . . Well, there were windows, but you couldn't be sure they would slide up and down properly.

Archie, an evil-looking scar-faced, scowling man of about forty-five, sat in the seat next to mine about midway in the bus. He was one of the last to join the crew and he'd stumbled and sidestepped his way over the human and inanimate litter in the aisleway and found the only available seat. There were no reserved seats on Rudy's bus. The Robinson family had assigned themselves to the seats near the front, but otherwise it was every man for himself. Archie had matter-of-factly, wordlessly, stowed his shopping bag full of belongings in one corner of a seat to use as a pillow, curled up like a fat yard dog, and gone immediately to sleep. Below him, the vehicle's dual rear tires were visible through a twelve-inch square hole in the floor boards. His big feet extended into the aisle as he slept and while he had my unqualified admiration for his indifference to the two exposed wheels directly underneath him, I can never forgive him for not having changed his socks. The foul stench of dirty footwear, old shoe leather, and the cumulative effects of many days—perhaps weeks—of Archie's bathlessness stank in my nostrils like something dead.

Little Virginia Lee Robinson tiptoed toward the rear of the bus, ballet-dancing artfully around the legs and bodies and baggage. The better to watch the passing panorama outside, she crawled carefully over the sleeping man in the seat across from mine. She was a slim, tiny girl for all of her seven years; but she was bright, animated, intensely curious.

Earlier that morning, as the sun had lifted itself out of the Atlantic to the east while Rudy Thompson's bus sped north on the highway, I had watched her gather scraps of newspaper from the floor and piece them together to read. She'd arranged the fragments on the seat beside her and spelled out in the headlines words that she knew. But she had soon tired of that game and with a cautious look at her sleeping mother and father, had crept silently to the back. I was the only other passenger awake. Rudy, the crew leader and driver, was busy with the task ahead of him. For me, the steady, insistent drone of the whirring wheels under Archie's seat made sleep impossible. I had dozed during the night, but by early dawn, with the sun spilling bright daylight through the open windows, I had given it up. Archie's steady foghorn snoring was fitting accompaniment to the whirring of the rolling tires under his seat.

At the open window Virginia Lee thrust her brown face into the breeze and drank in every sight, every detail. Her brushed, pig-tailed head bobbed up and down, back and forth, when something outside caught her fancy. Almost everything did. The bus jolted through acres and acres of sugar cane, then cornfields, then citrus groves and later, miles and miles of palmetto. Virginia Lee watched everything through the window of the speeding bus, and the magic and fantasy which exist only in a little child's mind were reflected on her shining face. I could imagine some of the questions that raced through her head: Who are those men out there in the field? What are they doing? Are they working, or resting, or playing soldier-at-war in the long columns of tall corn? What is that growing out there? There's so much of it. What will they do with all of it?

Virginia Lee was utterly fascinated. There was a tenderness and sweetness about her and one wanted to share in her games. For a time she counted telephone poles as the bus passed them by. She tolled them off, one after another, in a half-whispered singsong voice, consciously careful not to disturb anyone. She lost count though—at some point after one hundred and twenty-two—and then forgot about telephone poles. Once she saw a man changing a flat tire on his truck by the roadside and she watched him through the window as long as she could. A faint frown, perhaps of instinctive sympathy for the unknown man's ill fortune, fell, ever so fleetingly, across her brown face. She brightened quickly though, when the bus rattled over a long bridge. She counted aloud, pointing a finger at fishing boats tied up at a pier. She listened, head cocked to one side, to the changing tune of the tires as they hummed over the steel-mesh roadbed of the bridge underneath. Everything she saw became part of her adventure, and she was completely enthralled.

It was a long time before she became aware of me as an observer. She had busied herself at the games a little child plays. She had conducted mysterious, enchanting conversations with herself. From the window of the speeding bus she had discovered exciting new things. The rest of the crew of seventeen still slept. Fat little Adolphus, in a world of his own, slumbered comfortably in his mother's arms. But sleep was not for Virginia Lee. There was excitement outdoors.

I had not been invited to join her games, nor would I have dared to intrude, but suddenly she asked, "What's that, mister?" She pointed to a tall cylindrical building near a farmhouse a hundred yards off the road.

"It's a silo," I told her. "It's full of corn—or will be when the fields are harvested—to feed the pigs and cattle when it's cold."

She smiled a courteous thank you and said, "Oh, I know what they are. There was one on a farm where we lived once. My daddy and momma worked there."

Virginia Lee's slumbering seatmate rolled over in a subconscious search for a more comfortable spot for his huge frame. He muttered something unintelligible under his breath. Because Archie's big clod-hoppered feet changed position, too, the child had to find a new space for her knees. So she rested one bony leg on the seat and stretched the other one down to the floor. The temporary inconvenience wasn't really a bother, so she turned to the window again to drink in the passing scenery.

With her mother, her father and her little brother, Virginia Lee Robinson was on the way up the road on the season. It was her fourth or fifth trip with the traveling harvesters. She couldn't recall just which. For Adolphus it was the first journey. Robert Andrew and Mattie had long ago stopped counting their years on the season.

What was the use?

Both had been born on a migrant camp. So had Virginia Lee and Adolphus. They had only the haziest notion that there was another kind of life; that there was anything else to do than pick up the crops as long as they lasted, then load them into trucks and railroad cars and move along to another place where farm help was needed. Their world was circumscribed by crops to pick, bags and boxes and hampers to lift, mean ill-smelling shanties to live in and the landlord to be paid his money at the end of the week; and broken-down buses and trucks to haul them from one field to another. It was a futile existence, from which escape was possible but extremely difficult.

There was one eighteen-year-old boy, for example, who had migrated with his family from Florida to the apple and peach country of the Upper Hudson Valley in northern New York. He was one of the fortunate few who did get to elementary, junior and senior-high school at intervals during the seasons. An alert teacher had early detected brilliance in the boy and guided him to a college scholarship. As a result, the youth became a brilliant student at Syracuse University and captain and star of its championship football team. But such happy endings are rare.

Only by the sheerest of accidents would the Robinson family pause long enough in their travels to find time—and means—to enroll Virginia Lee at a full-fledged school, where perhaps another alert teacher might take note of her refreshing charm, her superior though unpolished intelligence and guide her into a better life. They are career migrants, all four of them: Robert Andrew, Mattie, bright-eyed Virginia Lee, and infant Adolphus. Their lives begin and end where the crops are.

The rest of the crew began to stir and awaken as the red-gold sun climbed higher into the sky. We were headed due north on a four-lane concrete highway, not far inshore from the Florida coast. Having picked the last of the Dade County tomato fields clean some three hundred miles to the south, we were on our way to more crops to harvest. The big bus that carried us there was only one of many that had coughed and sputtered out of Homestead the night before. Archie, on the seat opposite me, stretched and rubbed the sleep from his eyes. He untangled his legs, extended his feet into the aisle, and for the first time seemed to become aware of wheels below and of the concrete roadway clearly visible through the big hole in the flooring. When the crew leader guided the bus off on the graveled shoulders to afford a passing vehicle more space, the wheels dashed pebbles against the floor under Archie's seat. He had slept the night through ignoring the chatter of gravel, but now, fully awake, he began to show concern. . . .

Conversation with Archie—even with the little girl who, upon Archie's awakening had moved to the seat ahead—was all but impossible in the cacophony of whirring tires, the rattle of gravel, and the noisy awakening riders; so, I made my way to the front through the tangle of bodies and baggage.

A cigarette dangled from the corner of Rudy's mouth as he wheeled the reluctant, laboring bus up the highway. He managed the curves with skillful efficiency. He'd been driving all night, but he wound deftly in and out of the slow-moving traffic without a hitch. He handled the big vehicle with a sure touch, as though he were fingertip-reining a plowhorse around a race track; and he knew both his mount and the track equally well.

"Been goin' up the road a gang of years," he declared, turning to me and temporarily ignoring the on-coming traffic. "I'll be doin' it some more. Got this here bus from my daddy. He carried labor crews all the way up into Canada in this thing. I been doing the same thing."

Rudy was city-bred, born in Tampa, he said; and he showed it. He admitted that, except for occasional inconveniences experienced while hauling farm labor for hire from one place to another, he had always slept between sheets. That was one of the things that marked him as of a breed apart from his passengers. He was round-faced, smooth-shaven and well-fed. Even his speech was different. His language was that of the Deep South, but with a certain polish, a thin veneer of clipped tones, articulated prefixes and suffixes. There was no mistaking his birth and upbringing, but at the same time there was the distinct impression that he had been around. He wore a checked, Ivy League-style summer-weight cap that had only recently reposed on a shelf in some big-city haberdashery. His bleached-white tee shirt seemed to have been freshly laundered and the creases of newness were still visible in his tan chino pants. White tennis shoes branded him as clearly not of the field-labor class.

He lounged casually in the driver's seat, a nonchalant eye on the traffic, and I noted that his ample paunch spilled in a roll over his belt. Rudy was about thirty-five, and his arms and shoulders were thick-muscled and massive. He could literally have thrown a bull with his bare hands. His full, deep-throated voice was entirely consistent with his build; and he spoke in a perpetual shout above the roar of the engine and assorted rattles of his old bus.

"These here people"—he nodded at them over a shoulder—"is headed for the best deal they ever had. I haul them three hundred miles up the road and don't charge 'em a dime. Tell you the truth, they cost me money. Then I put 'em—every man and woman of 'em—to work at good wages. How ya gonna beat that? They didn't have nothing when they got on this bus; they ain't got nothing to lose. We're gonna start to work the minute we get there and they can all have money in their pockets by the end of the first day. A good hand can make himself 'round fifteen or twenty dollars, and nothin's gonna be taken out."

Rudy snorted the ashes from his cigarette without removing it from his mouth. He examined me intently from top to bottom and declared, "Boy, you look like a good hand. If you're smart, maybe I'll make you a checker or something, countin' the baskets—like that. Maybe you won't have to do no work in the fields. Can you count?"

I assured him that I could figure numbers as well as the next man, though I hadn't anything special in the way of schooling.

"That's good, boy," he bellowed. "I'll take care of you when we get to the end of the line."

On first talking with and listening to Rudy Thompson, it occurred to me that I had met him before, with other names, in other places—New York City, Chicago, Detroit—well, you name it. Clearly he was a man who knew the score, the kind of fellow who would always see to it that he remained ahead of the game; and, wherever possible, at odds heavily in his favor. Without ever asking him, without anyone's telling me, I knew him as a man addicted to soft, feminine, not-too-smart women—as many of them as he could find—good liquor and no-table-stakes poker with gamblers he was sure he could beat. That was the image he projected: self-confidence to the point of egomania, an awareness of his own animal attraction to women, and if you don't like it, goddam it, git outta the way.

He rolled his filter-tip cigarette around between his lips with studied casualness. He centered it in his mouth and bounced gusts of smoke against the windshield. When he was finished, he simply opened the air vent to his left and blew the butt out through it. Though he appeared superficially to be preoccupied with his own personal thoughts, his attention never really departed from the task at hand—steering the cumbersome bus through heavy traffic at maximum speed.

At last he wheeled off the concrete highway and jolted down a winding dirt road. Rows of corn and tomatoes stretched away at right angles to the narrow lane. There were few farmhouses in view, but many large structures—barns, equipment-storage buildings—rose in clearings between the broad fields. Occasionally the corn and tomatoes gave way to cabbage and snap beans. The green vegetables were just poking their way through the black soil. Some of the passengers noted the immaturity and there was a rumble of discontent all through the bus.

"Ain't none of these crops ready," one man declared.

"It'll be two or more weeks 'fore this stuff is big enough to pick," said another.

The crew boss said nothing. His attention was devoted to maneuvering the old vehicle around ruts and potholes into a clearing.

There were three rows of tin-and-tarpaper shanties by the side of the road, thirteen in all. The one on the end in the back row was in danger of crumbling to a heap of old rubbish. The winds had ripped the shingle roofing from three or four of the shanties and had blown the windows out of several more. An uneasy, unhealthy shroud of decay and abandonment hung over the camp. It appeared not to have been lived in for years. In the weed-grown back yard a well-digging apparatus, rusted and wind-bent, towered 50 to 60 feet overhead. Doors to the shacks had been boarded and nailed shut and the driveway leading into the clearing was overgrown with tall grass.

With a harsh clash of gears and grinding of brakes, Thompson brought the bus to a stop. He unwound from the driver's seat and got out. His eyes swept the deserted migrant-farm-labor camp as the crew of seventeen weary, hungry, road-tired harvesters tumbled out of the bus.

"Looks like there might be a little wait before there's work here to do," Rudy said to no one in particular. "Looks like this stuff ain't quite ready."

It was a monumental understatement.

Archie walked slowly, deliberately to the head of a row and wrenched a young cabbage plant out of the dirt. He peeled away the outer leaves and cupped the small head in the palm of his hand. It was about the size of a tennis ball. He tossed it lightly from one hand to another, then, with an oath, hurled it back to the earth.

"We got ourselves mixed up with another lyin', son-of-a-bitch crew boss," he swore, "an' ain't nothin' we can do about it. We're a long way from nowhere out here in these fields an' we're gonna be owin' that bastard for eatin' an' sleepin' long 'fo' these 'matoes an' cabbages is ready to pick. He was sure right about one thing—we didn't have nothin' when we got here. Well, we ain' gonna have nothin' when we leave neither."

This was the Utopia that Rudy Thompson had promised the evening before in his spiel from the milk-crate platform in Homestead's "colored town."

". . . work for anybody who wants to make money. Tomatoes and snap beans falling off the vines. So much cabbage to chop that you can't see to the end of the field," he'd told the folks clustered hopefully around him.

Sixteen—I was the seventeenth—blindly trusting souls that had heeded his pitch. There was at last an answer to Virginia Lee's question, the answer that her mother hadn't supplied: No, Virginia, there isn't any schoolhouse. It's like the last place and the one before. Maybe there would be a school at the next place. . . . "We'll see, honey. We'll see."

In my own naïveté I, had expected a good deal more than I saw at the abandoned labor camp. I had been prepared to believe Rudy Thompson when he promised comfortable beds and sleep every night between sheets. That was one of the reasons I had joined him. The day in the tomato fields near Homestead had not been exactly an easy time and I had every intention of watching the rest of this crew go about the work of gathering crops while I questioned them as I had Red Fisher. And I hoped to get answers. Had the sixteen travelers in Rudy's crew really been sold on his carnival pitch? Did they really expect to find the milk and honey he had said awaited all of us at the end of the road?

3

"They'll Beat You Half to Death"

The second of six vehicles in the crew leader's entourage arrived just after noon. It was a big, five-ton stake truck piled high with farm hands, harvest equipment, and spare parts. Four men sat abreast in the driver's cab, an undisguised violation of motor-vehicle laws, and after that came a jalopy station wagon and three passenger cars, loaded with harvesters. There had been recruiting for this grower's fields at other farm villages along the three hundred miles from Homestead and when the last road-weary passenger tumbled out of the last car, there were some forty men, women, and children wandering aimlessly around the compound.

The camp was nestled between two broad tomato fields.

The long, carefully laid rows stretched arrow straight toward the horizon almost as far as you could see. At regular intervals irrigation ditches broke the ledger-book pattern. It was easy to tell where the rows ended and the ditches began. Tall greenery and underbrush bordered each of the waterways. The wheels of tractors and cultivators had plowed furrows in the turn-arounds at the ends of the rows. Nothing grew in the ruts made by the wheels, but weeds and grass had sprung up between the wheel marks. Reaching away to the rear of the camp, perpendicular to the rows of tomatoes, was a rectangular field of corn. The fields were perfectly flat, and a light breeze rippled over the shoulder-high budding tassels like waves over a calm inland lake. You could see over the yellow blossoms to where the corn field ended several hundred yards away. An irregular row of pine trees lined both banks of a small stream.

To the left of the camp was a small concrete pumphouse. It appeared to have been newly erected. The structure was covered with green roofing shingles, but there were no windows, only a small padlocked door. It housed the irrigation pump and inside the building, behind the locked door, an engine chugged at its task regularly like a raucous metronome. Provisions had been made for adequate shelter for the irrigation pump, but something less than comfortable quarters had been furnished—or unfurnished—for the field hands brought there to gather the crops.

The clearing was about 100 yards square and on it were perched, in various states of decay and disrepair, three columns of four-in-a-row shanties. A thirteenth building stood alone and slightly apart from the others. It was nearest the corn fields to the rear. From the outside it appeared to be in somewhat better condition than the rest. It was not necessary that a sign be hung out in front of the shack. Without being told I knew it belonged to the bossman. Rudy had observed the night before, while wheeling his bus up the highway from the little farm town near the Keys, that he lived by a long-established, irrevocable rule. When at all possible, there must be maximum creature comfort in his quarters, no matter where, and for the paunchy, garrulous crew chief comfort began in a soft bed, between clean sheets. It was distinctly fetishist with him and perhaps it sprang from the same thought processes that propelled him in the direction of soft, feminine women—particularly submissive, pliable ones who gave him no trouble, asked him no questions. Somewhere in the recesses of the man's mind there was an affinity between the soft beds which he had made one of his habits and the species of woman that attracted him most.

Almost all of the windows in the row of shanties nearest the dirt road had been broken. In a few instances the windows had been boarded up and nailed tightly shut. There was no way for rain-freshened, sun-purified Florida air to penetrate the dank bowels inside. A strong wind, perhaps a hurricane off the Caribbean, had sometime in the past wrenched the corrugated sheet-metal roofing from the tops of the 14-by-16-foot shanties and the sheeting was upended and ragged in many places. Elsewhere big gaping holes in the roofs of the buildings exposed the wood beams underneath. Years ago, when an inexpert carpenter had thrown the structures together, undoubtedly even then as temporary shelter for harvesters, they had been covered wtih tarpaper. But that, too, had been ripped away in places by the winds and the naked pine boards were exposed to the elements.

The corner supports of some of the buildings had sunk into the soft sandy earth and they tilted off center. An ancient potbellied cookstove had been pressed into service at the corner of one shack to hold up the side. A metal milk crate propped up the corner of another. Three or four wooden steps led up to the front door of each shack. Weeds and tall grass had grown up around the steps. And a foul odor of decay and abandonment, with undertones of the invigorating scents of growing green vegetation, hung over the camp. The shuffling of feet and the angry grumbling of some crop pickers stirred up both the dust and the ugly atmosphere around the place.

There was no pot of gold at the end of this crew leader's rainbow. There were no dollar bills hanging on every tomato vine. The promised land up the road which Rudy Thompson had so vividly painted was, in the faded color of reality, only an unpromising, deserted farm-labor camp well off the main highway.

Robert Andrew Robinson unburdened himself of his family's belongings—the bedspread bundle of dirty laundry and the cardboard beer carton—and dumped them into a pile before one of the shanties. He led his wife, Mattie, the sleeping Adolphus in her arms, to a seat on the steps. Virginia Lee tagged along, carrying her rubber doll in one hand and clutching her tattered picture book in the other.

The sun angled obliquely over a corner of the camp clearing. The irrigation pump engine chugged with a mechanical, sometimes irregular tempo, spouting water through a large pipe to foam into a ditch on the way to the corn and tomato plants.

Robert leaned one shoulder against the wall of the cabin, thrust both hands into his pockets and eyed his family.

"Mattie," he said, "the bossman told us there ain't nothin' ready to pick here for a while. There ain't no food here neither, an' no stove to cook it on if we had some. Look like we got here too soon." He kicked a miniature furrow in the soft dirt, "We got to get somethin' to eat . . . an' quick!"

Mattie looked first at her husband, then at the baby. "That sure is the truth," she said. "He'll be mighty mean if I have no milk for him."

Adolphus stirred, rearranged himself more comfortably and went back to sleep. A crisis had been momentarily averted but it would come again.

To label Robert Andrew an easygoing man would be not to describe him at all. Superficially, the word would isolate one of his character traits. But there was more, much more, to him than gentle submissiveness. True, he was soft of nature, placid, easily led—or misled—and tractable to a fault.

What other manner of man would have bundled his family up at a moment's notice and blindly moved them and their beer-carton-bedspread baggage, to the dead end of a backwoods farm-labor camp?

Robert was slight of stature, almost boyishly built, with slim tapered upper body and a small waistline. He was just a few inches over five feet in height and weighed not over 135 pounds.

Yet, the man was wiry and tough. Corded muscles stood out in his lean neck when he moved his head around to survey the tiny patch of the world around him. Strong, sun-blackened arms showed through his rolled-up-to-the-biceps shirtsleeves. There was every evidence that he had spent many long days at hard labor.

He was a man who, it appeared, existed for the purpose of being taken advantage of by others; but there was nothing in his manner which suggested the bitterness, the rancor which touched other men of his kind. He was a man to be told what to do—and he did it. He could be told what not to do—and he shunned it. He never entertained the thought that an order, even a suggestion, could operate to his disadvantage. It mattered only that he had been told what to do and he did, or did not, do it. His slim, youthful face was open and innocent, almost like that of a child. Every emotion, every thought, every fear—and every delight—was candidly inscribed upon his chocolate countenance. This, perhaps, was the reason that Mattie had married him. Beyond a doubt (it was clear in her tired eyes) she loved him. In the few short hours since we had met at the "loading grounds" in Homestead, I found that I had developed a special regard for him, too. Robert was truly an honest man; a man who knew nothing of vindictiveness.

I hunkered in the powdery dirt in the Robinson family circle. Roly-poly Adolphus still slept in his mother's arms, completely oblivious to all that went on around him. It was just as well. Occasionally he puckered his lips in the instinctive search of the young for a mother's breast. After a while Mattie allowed him to nurse.

The adventure of arriving at a new place overwhelmed Virginia Lee. She clung to her doll baby and her picture book as she took in the new sights. Her wide eyes left nothing unexplored. Everything in her view was a new source of amazement, an exciting discovery. She inspected the broken-down shanties, from the outside of course, and the rusting, wind-bent well digger. She listened to the ceaseless, irregular chugging of the irrigation pump.

She asked many questions of the people around her; and she was not very often satisfied with the answers she got, if she got any at all.

"Who's going to live here? Where are the other kids my momma said would be here? Where do we have to play?"

The little girl was most unlike her father. She accepted nothing at face value. Everything was to be scrutinized. The unfathomable was to be investigated.

There was one question she wanted to ask, but she didn't dare. It formed on her lips, then faded, unarticulated: Where was that school that momma said might be here?

The truth was that the child knew the answer. She had seen enough of the camp; she realized its remoteness; she knew it was abandoned, deserted. It would be the same as the last place, and the one before that. There was to be no school.

The little girl had been conditioned to disappointments and though this one hurt a little bit more than the others, she had cultivated (perhaps inherited) the rare kind of fortitude which helped her to shed the heartbreaks. She did not permit them to destroy her dreams.

The little girl broke away from the family group, head hung and silent, and shuffled around a corner in search of another part of the clearing to explore.

Her mother breathed an audible sigh of relief as she watched the child scuff through the dirt in her bare feet. She hadn't wanted to face the question; now the inevitable answer could be postponed for a while.

The flame-red sun settled over the camp's shoulder into the trees and it became increasingly clear to Robert that the immediate problem was food. The crew leader had vanished somewhere in one of the trucks and there was muted grumbling and disorganized stirring about the camp as the men and women, and a few children, wandered aimlessly between the rows of cabins in search of somewhere to settle down.

There was no food about the place. The cabins were in no way ready for occupancy. Except for the irrigation pump, there was no water supply; nor were there toilets or other sanitary facilities. The last inhabitants of the camp had left the place in disarray, with miscellaneous debris and litter scattered around the shanties.

Robert dug a two-pound Maxwell House coffee can ("It's good to the last drop!") out of a mountain of equipment in the rear of one of the crew leader's trucks. He scooped a shallow hole in the dirt with a broken-handled hoe he found under one of the shanties. With brush and leaves and bits of paper, he built a fire in the hole, then placed four discarded vegetable tins at each corner. Over them he laid a rectangular sheet of metal roofing which he had found somewhere in the clearing.

Robert went about his task purposefully, methodically, as though he had a plan. Mattie watched as though she had seen it all done before. I watched with quiet amazement.

Despite all of his shortcomings, Robert was a resourceful man and that quality reinforced my own regard for him.

Dry wood and brush soon blazed under the sheet-metal roofing and Robert walked down the dirt road leaving the fire in his makeshift open-air stove to grow hotter. A few moments later he returned with two cabbages which he had torn from their roots in a nearby field.

He filled the coffee-can cookpot with water from the irrigation pump, then with his pocketknife, cut one of the cabbages into bite-size pieces and dumped them into the can. He placed it carefully on the stove and squatted beside it to wait.

After a time the hot water softened the unsalted cabbage and it was ready, as ready as it ever would be—the first meal for the Robinson family since they'd departed Homestead many hours—and more than three hundred miles—earlier.

Robert lifted the infant from his mother's arms to give her the first turn at the cookpot. With the pocketknife he had handed her she speared a few chunks of cabbage and put them into her mouth. She rolled them around for a moment, then began chewing slowly, reluctantly, hesitantly. At last she gave the pocketknife back to her husband.

Mattie Robinson had been weary when she climbed into Rudy Thompson's crew bus in Homestead, but now I saw a human being completely consumed by discouragement. She brushed her knotted, early-gray hair back with her hands as she fought with all the courage she could muster to hold back the tears. She locked her fingers tightly behind her back and looked away from her husband.

She pondered her plight: a long trip to nowhere, to poverty and hunger amid plenty. It was the way it had been before; it was the way it was now; it was the way it would be tomorrow.

This was the way of a migrant farm family.

At last the woman wept silently. Great tears welled up in her eyes, rolled heavily down both dark cheeks, and collected in pools in the wrinkles at the sides of her mouth. When the baby began to cry, she bent to take him from his father, and the tears fell onto the hot sheet-metal cookstove he had built.

Mattie didn't notice where her tears fell; she didn't hear them sizzle and dance and sputter away. She still wept silently, and a shudder began at the top of her head and fell like a dark shroud down over the length of her tired, sagging body.

Robert was unaware of his wife's fleeting confrontation with despair. He had been busy spearing pieces of boiled cabbage with his right hand while holding his son in his left arm.

That was the kind of man he was—and Mattie loved him.

Behind the battered Chevrolet in the clearing there was now an ancient jalopy station wagon. It was of pre-World War II vintage and it appeared to have been caught in the crossfire of one of that campaign's major engagements. Doors hung awry and fenders were dented and misshapen. What was left of the paint was cracked and peeling. The rear folding tailgate had been banged into a grotesque mass of twisted steel. The handle had been lost long ago in some past collision and a length of heavy twine bound the gate to the doorframe. Two passenger automobiles, of indefinite age and indifferent lineage, and a big flat-bed truck were parked behind the wagon.

The last arriving vehicle of the convoy was the surprise element. One of Rudy Thompson's field bosses had driven it up from Homestead and he had been duly cautioned at threat of death to handle it with fastidious care. It was, like the soft beds and sheets, one of the luxuries the crew boss lavished upon himself and it was to be regarded with the same kind of reverence that its owner had for it. It was a silver metallic Buick sedan and it boasted a superfluity of chrome trim like a twentieth-century chariot. It was, indeed, an auto-accessory dealer's delight. It bore radio antennae both front and rear and from each of them hung a long, streaming tassel of iridescent shocking pink plastic which danced in the winds off the corn fields.

A rear bumper extension gave the automobile additional length and bulk, and built into the chrome-covered assembly was a customized spare tire mounting which added still more to the vehicle's elongation. Inside, the car had all of the trappings of a department-store window display. Bright red upholstery covered the front and rear seats, and a film of protective transparent plastic had been tailored over the seat covers. Fluffy red carpeting covered the floors and a strip of red, tasseled trimming—in keeping with the over-all color scheme—had been stitched around the inside of the rear window. Mouth ajar and teeth flashing, a three-foot-long stuffed baby-alligator carcass was stretched out across the rear-window deck.

This was the crew leader's personal transportation. It had been decorated in the flamboyant manner to which he had accustomed himself during the years he had hauled farm labor crews up and down the road to the harvests. He had been careful to circulate the word around camp that no one was to lay a smudgy hand or breathe a hot breath upon it.

The car proclaimed Rudy Thompson's personality in a

way that nothing else could: it was big; it was loud; it was shiny and superficial.

At a respectful distance away from the crew leader's chariot, Archie Rollins, the man with the stinking feet, had gathered a cluster of grumbling malcontents about him. He was an outspoken man, and he said what he meant. He said it often and in indelicate language. He was sturdily built, weighed about 200 pounds, and stood perhaps an inch or a fraction thereof over six feet. A fringe of black hair half-circled his big round head. His waistline measured at least 50 inches. He was one of the more affluent members of the labor crew, since he wore a wristwatch, and he consulted it frequently between emphasizing points in his rapid-fire monologue of all that was wrong with working—or not working—with the Rudy Thompson crew.

"This makes," he declared, "the ninety-ninth time I been lied to by a son-of-a-bitch crew boss. He said we'd be workin' the minute we got here. He said there'd be blankets an' sheets. That bastard said we'd be picking 'matoes and cabbages out of the fields like they was dollar bills.

"What we got? We ain't got a goddam thing. We ain't got nothin' but that bastard's bullshit."

Archie consulted his status-symbol timepiece, glowered at the lowering sun again and listened a moment to the muttered assents of his audience.

"An' he got us 'way out here in this woods and we can't git to no place." He jabbed a finger into a man's face and demanded, "You got any money to get anyplace?"

The man fingered the miscellanea in his pockets, squinted toward Archie, and agreed that he was without funds.

"Jus' about like every man here," he remarked. "I'm dead busted. Ain't got a cent. Didn't come here with nothin' an' it don't look like I'll have nothin' when I leaves."

Archie's lament was the same dissonant tune I heard over and over again, like a blues refrain, in weeks of living and working and traveling with migrant farm laborers. It was the way they were swept up in the migrant stream; it was the way many of them spent their lives. There was little chance of escape. They were induced by magnanimous promises to follow the crew bosses on their trips to a land of milk and honey. At the end of the line they find that the milk is curdled and the honey soured.

What weaknesses, what aberrations, what quirks move a man to succumb again and again to the same false promises of good pickin's up the road?

Archie, his anger momentarily spent, his indignation fully declared, relaxed a while later in the settling dusk and in candor provided some of the answers. He lit a cigarette, focused the glow of the paper match on his wrist watch to illuminate the dial and said, "One of these trips up the road I'm going to find me a good man to work for. He's going to pay me every dime he owes me and he's going to give me a good place to sleep and eat. For that man I'll work extra hard. I'm a good hand in the fields. Been doing it most of my life. Know how to pick 'matoes and snap beans and the rest of the crops. C'n do it better than most. Never had no schoolin' and I can't write my name. But that don't stop me from puttin' in a good day's work. I want to get my money on payday, though. I ain't asking for no more than that.

"Heard tell of folks who went on the season and caught hold of something good someplace and stayed there. Me, I always wanted to get up north someplace and catch hold of something. Ain't nothing for me in Florida. Had to get out. So I came with this man, Rudy. Thought maybe he was the one I been lookin' for. Thought he meant what he said. It looks like he didn't, don't it? One of these days I'll catch a good one to work for. There's got to be some of 'em around somewhere. I got to latch onto one sooner or later. So I keep on travelin' and tryin'. Trouble is, when I get up the line to the end of the road I ain't never had 'nough money to stay there. Always got to come back and start again.

"Got in trouble in South Carolina once. Had a fight with a man an' he got himself killed. It was me or him, but the judge didn't see it that way. Gave me some jail time and that's on my record. They said it was manslaughter, whatever that is. I didn't do no more than look out for myself. Got in a fight with that man 'bout a woman I knew and first thing you know we was beatin' on each other's head. I got to a piece of lumber 'fore he did and that's the way the thing ended up. I tell you, man, it was him or me. But the judge didn't see it that way.

"Ain't had no trouble since. Don't aim to. But that's on my record an' I can't get no steady work. Can't find nothing to do but farm labor—pickin' the crops. Nobody don't ask me no questions in the fields. So I keep tryin' to find me a bossman who's going to pay me my wages on payday and treat me like a man ought to. I don't ask for no more than that.

"One of these days I'll get up the road and I'll find me some work and stay there. Always wanted to live up north. Hear tell the bossman don't cheat you so much. They pay you what they tell you they will. I jus' keep on movin' 'till I find what I'm lookin' for; then I ain't goin' on the season no more."

With Archie, strong, able-bodied, honest, but illiterate, it was the combination of the man he had beaten to death by the side of a road in the past, along with a dream of the future, that kept him moving from crop to crop and from season to season up the road. He had no assurance that his luck would ever steer him in the direction of a good man to work for. There was no guarantee that he would ever find anything good to hold on to up north. He was one soldier in the vast legion of farm workers who never escape the migrant stream. Very likely Archie was incapable of lifting himself out of the current and wading ashore to solid ground. He had killed a man and he had paid for it by serving out his time in prison. There simply was no escape for the scar-faced man. He would have to live with the bitterness he nursed inside.

Robert Andrew owed his migrancy to something different; yet he was trapped just as hopelessly, stooped over in the fields, gathering the harvest for somebody else; accepting the crumpled few dollars and change that the bossman handed him at the end of the day. He was a tiny, insignificant bit of flotsam caught in the swirls and eddies of the migrant stream. His life, like his son's, had begun in a farm-labor camp hidden away in the woods and he'd spent all of his thirty-odd years moving along from crop to crop on the way up the road. When the season was over at the end of the line, he traveled along with his folks back to Florida, or Georgia, or one of the tiny, nameless farm hamlets in the Carolinas, and when the tomatoes were ready, he started all over again. It was not in his character to throw himself into the face of the tide. The fewest demands were made upon him when he drifted along directionlessly—with one crew leader in need of cabbage choppers in one field; with a man who wanted hands to lift crates of tomatoes in another. Robert's chances of escape were nonexistent. He knew nothing of any other kind of life and seemed not to interest himself in learning. What lay on the other side of the camp, beyond the fields he happened to be laboring in at the moment, was another world which he had no inclination to explore. It was, he believed, hostile and foreign; it was, in his clouded view, a distant place of innumerable mysteries, all of them incomprehensible to him. Robert, like many of his fellow workers in the legion of stoop workers, was a victim of the itinerant harvester's syndrome.

Perhaps it will *not* be the same for Robert's little girl, Virginia Lee. Maybe by accident, rather than design, the family will find in its directionless movements from one crop to another a location where there are adequate educational facilities. Perhaps there will be a teacher somewhere who can answer the bright youngster's questions though her parents cannot. Perhaps there will come a time in Mattie Robinson's life when she can say, "Yes, Virginia, there is a school," when the little girl asks, "Momma, will there be a school where we're going? Will there? Huh, momma?"

It would at least point the child in the direction of escape from the migrant stream; it would be an advantage her parents had not had. Perhaps it will come as a result of enlightened attitudes of state and federal officials, and the realization that a large segment of the American population has been too long forgotten.

Sleep for the haggard, road-weary band of farm workers and the crew leader's handful of field bosses, motor-vehicle drivers, and assorted aides came relatively easy the first night at the camp. Doors and windows to the cabins had to be crow-barred open to gain entry, as well as to permit fresh air inside. The floors were littered with leaves and dust that the winds had blown in through the cracks, and the dried-up cadavers of flies and crickets were scattered—feet up—on the sills of the few windows that had glass in them. The insects had died, perhaps of asphyxiation, in their futile attempts to escape the prisonlike cabins. Most of the buildings were furnished with iron cots and moldy cotton mattresses, but there were no blankets or sheets.

I followed Archie's example and lay down fully clothed on one mattress and pulled a second one over me, like a coverlet. I had stowed my shopping bag carrier under my bed and piled my shoes on top of it, on the theory that a thief in the night would sound an alarm by dumping the big clodhoppers onto the pine-board floor.

The rumble of discontent awakened me early the next morning. In addition to Archie, there were four other men in my cabin. The talk was of no work, no pay, and attitudes toward the crew boss were uniformly contemptuous. As a newly initiated migrant farm worker I had given Rudy the benefit of the doubt. I had allowed for a miscalculation in timing; half believed that, indeed, he had not known the crops were not ready. My first thoughts had been charitable ones. But after listening to more of the interchange between the other stoop workers I found that I could not have been more mistaken. It wasn't a delay in the weather, as Rudy had insisted when he unwound and tumbled out of the bus, or that the corn and tomatoes, the snap beans and cabbage, were behind schedule. The grim truth was that the crew boss and the grower with whom he had a contract to harvest the fields had arranged the timetable exactly that way. It was an ancient gimmick that farm-labor contractors use everywhere—and have used since the beginning of time—to exploit the illiterate, inarticulate laborers. Hang them up, with their wives and families, at an out-of-the-way migrant camp from which they can't run and, since they don't have the wherewithal to pay their way, write them down in the books for food and lodging. There was no way they could earn any wages until the crops were ready, and even my inexperienced appraisal told me that none of them would be mature for ten days or more. It meant that the crew would stay on and on, running up debts on the boss-man's books, with the grower and, if they could arrange credit terms, with the general store a couple of miles down the road. Being in hock to someone, all of the time, was a way of life with many migrant farm workers, and the conditions into which Rudy Thompson's fat promise had led us were not unknown to the veterans of other similar experiences. The only thing to do was work off the debts when the crops came in, then move on up the road somewhere else. When the time came, Rudy would make the deductions for each worker whose name appeared on his books, then dole out, one by one, the few coins—if any—that were left.

The crew boss's timetable didn't mesh with mine. When I joined his corps of crop-pickers I had every intention of beginning work the first day after arrival at camp. I expected to be bent over in a field at the head of a row of snap beans, along with the others who had rumbled over the many bone-jarring miles on the trip up the road.

"You might as well loaf here as down there," Rudy told me when I asked the reason for our arrival well ahead of the crops. "There wasn't no work downstate and none of y'all was making no money. I'll see that you get some bread and beans after a while, and maybe some sandwiches. Pretty soon we'll get the kitchen set up."

Not only was the kitchen unready, but the well-digging rig brought in to tap the water supply for cooking and bathing seemed to have been abandoned the season before, with its work far from complete. The drill bit had been driven some distance into the earth, but the equipment appeared to have been left by its operator who went to lunch sometime the year before and never came back. The tall derrick was rusted from exposure and neglect.

Another thing that puzzled me was that there were no separate living quarters for men and women, and there were no sanitary facilities of any kind. The nearest toilet, for both males and females, was somewhere in the woods; and those who felt the need to wash the road dust off their hands and faces queued up and waited their turn at the irrigation pump.

As the morning wore on, it appeared that the crew chief's promise of bread and beans—and maybe some sandwiches—was as empty as his others had been. He was more concerned with inventorying his equipment and vehicles than in taking care of the help. Archie, one of the hardiest in the lot, proceeded to take matters into his own hands. He was a resourceful individualist. He found a packet of fishhooks somewhere in the miscellanea in his shopping bag. He ferreted a few feet of line out of the mountains of gear which Thompson's drivers had brought in on the truck and then he headed down the dirt road.

"That bastard crew boss ain' stud'n' about these people that's hungry," he spat over his shoulder. "Ain' no tellin' when he'll make any 'rangements for food. I'm goin' git me my own." And he did.

He returned to the clearing a few hours later with a half-dozen fresh-water fish on a string. I didn't wait around to find out what he did with them, but my brief acquaintance with the big man with the ugly scar on one cheek led to the conclusion that his discovery of a stream down the road with fish in it meant that at least one of the restive, ill-humored workers wouldn't starve.

I was keenly aware that a departure from camp would have to be arranged with caution. Rudy was the kind of man who would view without sympathy any desertions from his crew, particularly when he had made an investment in transporting us on a three-hundred-odd mile trip. Sticking around was part of the bargain. The fee was never specified, but talk around the compound had it that the charge might range from \$3 to \$5. It was understood that a certain amount of money for provisions would be exacted from each hand on the first payday. I was, perhaps, the most fortunate of all of Rudy's assemblage. I had an emergency fund tucked away in a money belt. I could either pay whatever he demanded or make it the best way I could to the nearest means of public transportation. I chose the latter.

"Walk away from this camp, boy," one of his field bosses told me, "and the cops in town will beat you half to death! If they don't catch you, me or Rudy will come after you ourselves. You didn't come here on no free ride," he added, "so you got to work 'til you pays off everything you owes. We ain't stupid, boy! You got to pay 'fore you leaves this camp."

The warning was ominous. He was a mean-looking fellow, lean and well over six feet. But I was determined to take my chances. I had heard the man make the same threats to other grumbling workers when it had become clear soon after our arrival that there would be no immediate work and no pay. Anyone who objected too loudly was threatened with head-whippings. That was the surest way to insure discipline in a disorganized, dissident crew. Though I didn't see anyone beaten, there was not the slightest doubt in my mind that Rudy, or one of his aides, would take whatever measures they thought necessary to make their point. The field boss' message came across clear to me. The threat strengthened my decision to leave and in the half-light before dawn I tucked my shopping-bag clothes carrier under my arm, eased out of the cabin in my stocking feet, and legged it along the road—three miles—to the nearest town.

I waited three hours at a gasoline service station for the first bus to Tampa. The others—they numbered about thirty-nine men, women, and a few children—were stranded out there in the woods, and they probably stayed on waiting and waiting and waiting, getting deeper in debt, until the crops came in. Then, back on the road, on the season.

For me, a good meal and a night's rest at a Tampa hotel offered welcome respite from the uncertainties at the camp. It was at the same time an opportunity to chart a course for the upstate Florida potato belt, where I had been told there was work to do, every day.

4

The Heavy Load

"What you want, boy?" Tony demanded impatiently when I confronted him at the work bench that served as his command post. I had applied for employment at a most inappropriate time.

Tony—Mr. Anthony Richard Norton—was boss of the big potato-grading and packing establishment I went to in search of a job almost immediately after hopping off the Greyhound bus in the gloomy little down-at-the-heels wide place along the highway in the heart of the North Florida potato country. It was Tony's job to crack the whip, like a backwoods Dixie-plantation overseer, over the crew of about thirty-five graders, truckers, loaders, washers, and general hand (and back) laborers who kept 100-pound sacks of potatoes flowing out of the open-air, tin-roofed processing shed for loading into railroad boxcars and trailer trucks and shipment to market, wherever that happened to be.

Convoys of flatbed stake trucks hauled the dirty brown root vegetables up the village's seedy, colorless main drag; past the movie house that featured an E-grade, low-budget Western with a horror show; past the general merchandise store that sold just about everything a farm family needed; and around the corner from the three-story brick town-meeting house to the grader where sweating, swearing, hard-muscled hoisters and lifters dumped them into washers. They tumbled around inside the mechanism until they were presentable enough for handling. Then they were disgorged onto moving belts and carried along breast-high conveyors to work counters where the women members of the crew hand-sorted them for quality and size.

Just at the moment when I approached Tony's work bench his ear had caught a troublesome note in the clattering of the pulleys and belts that drove the shed-enclosed machinery, and that was one of the reasons I seemed to be in the way.

Tony was in his early forties and already he was completely bald. When he took off his straw hat, his pate glistened under the naked electric bulbs hung in various places under the tin roof and when he stepped outside in the sun, droplets of perspiration glistened on his skull. He maintained a perpetual surveillance of every detail in his domain and his finely trained ear could detect an impending breakdown in the noisy machinery long before it occurred. He dashed nervously from one place to another, much like an artillery commander directing a company of troops. He scrawled entries hurriedly on a fiber clipboard which he carried under his arm, and he was all the time worrying for fear the goddam rattling machinery would suddenly, insolently, fly apart.

"What you want, boy?" he demanded again, when he saw me still standing around. In the properly respectful hat-in-hand tone which is accorded a white boss man in a hiring mood in the Deep South, I replied that I had only recently set foot in his little village, having come from Tampa on the strength of somebody's word that there was work to be had and wouldn't he please give me something to do. I was broke, I told him, and hungry, and needed work badly. I assured Mr. Tony that I was able-bodied and sound of limb; and that I was capable of any assignment he might be gracious enough to throw my way.

"It's hard work around here, boy," he warned, taking no note of the fact that I was well into my thirties, just a few years younger than himself, and he repeated, with emphasis, "It's hard work here and it's a ten-hour day, sometimes longer when there's a rush to get railroad cars out. If you ain't ready to do what you're told and keep at it 'till I tell you to stop, there ain't no place for you here."

I solemnly pledged to Mr. Tony, sir, that I was quite able to pull my own weight and ask for no quarter; that I had learned early in life that the thing to do on a white man's job was just what he said to do until he said I could stop. The affected, somewhat burlesqued façade of subservience appeared to convince Mr. Tony and he gave me permission to report on the job the first thing the next morning. Actually, he gave me the job somewhat against his best judgment. He had reservations: first, he wasn't sure I could handle the heavy labor called for at the grader; and next, he wasn't sure of my motivation in applying for work at his particular establishment. I had a story ready for him, but he didn't press and I didn't volunteer.

Work began at the grader promptly at eight o'clock. At that hour the chief engineer in charge of machinery pushed a button which sounded a whistle signaling the start of work. He pushed another button a moment later which set the belts and pulleys and conveyors into clanking motion. The rattling machinery set up such a furor that it discouraged conversation and, presumably, freed each worker's mind for production.

At the first blast of the whistle, just after sun-up on the morning I started, a dozen or so loaded trucks had already lined up in the driveway before the potato-washing apparatus, waiting for things to get under way. Stoop workers, some of them children, were already bending to their tasks in the fields surrounding the town, grubbing potatoes out of the earth and dumping them into the 100-pound burlap bags which they dragged or carried or pushed along ahead of them in their rows. Some of the loaded trucks had been left over from the day before.

Machine-grading potatoes is a production-line operation, perhaps one of the earliest points of instrusion of automation into the agricultural process. The first step begins when teams of hoisters hurl the nearly full, 80 to 100-pound bags into a washing apparatus. That was the lifters' assignment—for $1.00 an hour—from eight o'clock on any given morning when the chief engineer pushed the starting button, until day's end when the pulleys and belts and conveyors clanked to a halt.

It is dirty, grimy, monotonous work; it is hard, punishing labor any way it is sliced. Within a half hour after the unloading teams begin their work, they are encrusted with a film of sweat and field dust. It works its way into their pores and under their fingernails; it gets into their hair and eyes. There is no escape from it. If a man pauses for a moment to mop the gritty dirt from his face with a shirt sleeve, it is back again a few minutes later. The combination of steaming hot water under high pressure and the agitated tumbling of the potatoes in the machine's guts washes them reasonably clean, but the procedure is harder than hell on the men who labor to keep the thing running.

A chain belt moves the potatoes out of the washer and along work counters where women sort them for size, assigning No. 1 potatoes to the No. 1 conveyor; No. 2 potatoes to the No. 2 conveyor, and so on along the scale. It is their job, too, to pick out and discard the pieces and fragments which have been chopped up by the machinery. The women go to work at the same time as the men, but they earn considerably less money. The wage rates for female inspector-graders vary from place to place and from one part of the harvest season to another. The pay also depends upon the prevailing market price for potatoes. The hourly rate can be as little as 40 cents at season's end, for ten or more hours of dirty, grimy, sweaty work in the clamor and noise of a hot summer day; at season's peak it can reach the astronomical rate of 70 cents an hour.

After the potatoes are moved past the women graders, the conveyor channels them to a mechanical weighing device. It can be set at various calibrations—to weigh 10, 25, 50, or 100 pounds of potatoes for packaging, but it is not always accurate. Another two-man team, stationed at the terminal point of the conveyor system, runs each sack through a high-speed stitcher which binds it up at the top. Every fourth or fifth sack is checked on balance scales before it is stitched—to assure that no short-weight or overweight sacks are shipped—and potatoes are added or taken away as needed to bring the weight as near as possible to specifications.

Because each step in the grading process depends on another, there is no time for breaks. If one link in the production line is interrupted for any reason, the whole process slows down or stops. The man in charge of the machinery races through the shed, looking frantically for the cause of the trouble. It is time for Mr. Tony to worry about his production allotment and the schedule for loading railroad cars or trucks. Once Tony and the machine operator determine that a mechanical failure will last an extended period of time—more than an hour—the crew is dismissed and pay time halted. The work stoppage reaches all the way down the line, to the hoisters who dump sackfuls of potatoes into the washing apparatus, to the drivers who truck them from the fields to the grader, to the stoop workers who pick them up out of the dirt.

If a mechanical failure is protracted at the grader, virtually all of the work and almost all of the pay ends. It is reasonable to assume that the boss and his machine operator and perhaps a skeleton crew remain on the payroll, but the rank and file of migrant field and processing help are out of luck. Neither unemployment insurance nor workmen's compensation apply to agricultural laborers in the State of Florida. The harsh truth is that only the State of Hawaii and the Commonwealth of Puerto Rico specifically include agricultural workers under unemployment-insurance laws. In Puerto Rico, coverage of farm workers is restricted to the sugar industry, and they are protected to the same degree as are other workers. In Hawaii, all farm workers are covered if they are employed by a grower who has twenty or more employees on his payroll for twenty or more weeks in a calendar year. All other states exclude agricultural workers from unemployment as well as health and accident insurance; the District of Columbia has no farm workers within its borders. The laws of all but three states—Alabama, Massachusetts, and New York—permit voluntary extension of unemployment and sick and accident insurance, but few states have taken advantage of the elective provisions of the law.

The plight of farm laborers who are injured or killed while at work—or while in transit to or from work—is far more dismal than that of those laid off because of crop or mechanical failure, lack of work, or inclement weather. Workmen's compensation was one of the first pieces of social legislation developed in the United States—in Wisconsin in 1911, with ten other states quickly following. But only seventeen states have enacted laws which afford farm workers any coverage at all. And only eight of these states, and the Commonwealth of Puerto Rico have extended such statutory coverage to agricultural workers in the same manner as others. Of these nine laws, eight are compulsory. In Vermont under an elective statute, farm workers are covered unless employers choose in writing to withhold benefits in the event of injury or death. The New Jersey law, also elective, has been interpreted as being broad enough to apply to farm workers. Puerto Rican contract workers, under the persistent pressure of the Commonwealth's Labor Department Migration Division, have the same benefits as do factory workers. In a few states (Arizona, Kentucky, Louisiana, Minnesota, New York, Oklahoma, South Dakota, and Wyoming) farm workers who operate certain kinds of equipment—such as baling and threshing machines—are covered by workmen's compensation laws and in some of these states the law is compulsory. The Louisiana law, however, specifically writes farm workers out of its coverage while they are being hauled to and from work, no matter in what kind of carrier.

"Grab that there hand truck," Mr. Tony commanded when I appeared on schedule for work. "See about getting them sacks of potatoes off the grader and into them boxcars. You just fall in line with the other boys and do what they do. I'll give you a trial for a while and see how you do. If you don't keep that hand truck moving 'till I tell you to stop, I'll fire you before you can open your mouth. Now, get to it!"

General Norton turned his attention again to his command post. His flashing blue eyes reconsidered the deployment of troops in the grader and he made mysterious entries in his clipboard. He had not asked my name, nor had he inquired of my work experience. He had not asked for my Social Security number, nor had he shown any interest in my address, telephone number, or next of kin to be notified in case of accident.

The assignment before me was clear. The job was to station my truck at a point near the mechanical stitching device where a crew loaded it with four 100-pound sacks of potatoes. Then I was to wheel the truck approximately 150 feet along a board platform, up an inclined metal ramp and into a railroad car. There, another team of hoisters and hurlers would snatch the sacks off my truck and stack them floor-to-ceiling inside the boxcar.

There is a special technique in negotiating a heavily loaded hand truck over 150 feet of uneven plank flooring, then pushing it up a 20-degree ramp. The trick is to balance the load over the wheels adroitly, so that the labor is performed by the weight, not one's muscles and back.

The easiest way is to tip the handles ever so slightly forward so that the weight is just ahead of the wheels. The arms and shoulders apply just the right balance and forward motion, but it is the precise load distribution over the wheels that gets the work done.

It was not a difficult assignment to master and I maintained my place in the line along with nine other hand truckers for more than half a day. Ten trips. Twenty trips. Fifty trips. Then I lost count of the number of journeys along the uneven board platform and up the incline into the cars.

The only rest periods occurred during the few minutes it took the loaders and unloaders to perform their roles in the routine. It was just enough time to light a cigarette, take a few puffs, then jog along in the line with the rest of the truckers.

It was tedious, monotonous, laborious—for a dollar an hour.

Tony worried incessantly about keeping his grader machinery in operation. Except for brief pauses for adjustments, the motors and pulleys and belts clattered and spat out the 100-pound bags with clocklike precision. The air all about the grader was thick and oppressive with a mixture of dust and fragments of potato skins stirred up by the washing apparatus, and clouds of moisture which escaped through breaches in the contraption.

Suddenly Tony paused near the weighing device, mopped his bald pate with a handkerchief and commanded: "Y'all boys got to get five sacks off the grader every load from now on, 'stead of four. The yard engine is fixin' to move the boxcars someplace else and we got to get 'em loaded, raht now!"

The word passed along from one man to another in the line of truckers and there was mutinous grumbling directed at Mr. Tony. But there was no break in the pace. The order to increase the load—to one-quarter of a ton—had not been unexpected. No additional time was allowed to make the long trip along the platform. It was pick up your hand truck when it was loaded and get the hell out of the way for the next man. It meant that the sweat came a little more quickly and it became a little more difficult to balance the load at just the right point ahead of the wheels. It meant, also, applying a little more muscle when hustling the load up the incline. But you did what the bossman told you to do until he said you could stop—or you went somewhere else to look for work and somebody else took your place.

Junior was a young fellow in the line of hand-truck jockeys. He was just past his mid-teens, but he was wiry and tough for his slender build and he kept pace with the older, bigger, stronger men in the crew. In fact, I learned from him the most efficient way to handle my own load. All morning he trotted along the platform just ahead of me, pushing his truck into the railroad car being loaded, then back again to get four 100-pound sacks of potatoes which the team in charge of the stitching machine stacked neatly on his two-wheeled potato rig. Junior brought all of the exuberance of youth to the job. He was disrespectfully brash with the older men and teased some of them who were slower than himself. He was performing a man's labor and he demanded to be treated accordingly.

Toward the late afternoon, though, the youngster began to lag. He stopped more frequently to light cigarettes and he paused often—his eyes carefully cocked in the direction of Mr. Tony—for no other reason than to catch his breath. He blew his nose when it didn't need it, and his trips to the men's room were closer together and of longer duration than anyone else's.

The bossman's order to boost the size of the load was beginning to take its toll. Now and then Junior rolled his loaded truck out of the column and bent over to inspect an already tied shoelace, or to make believe he was extracting a splinter that was not under his fingernail. They were clearly delaying tactics and for a time he thought he was getting away with something. The crisis came when the boy misguided his truck up the ramp and ran it off the edge of the platform instead of into the boxcar. Five hundred pounds of potatoes, along with the truck, crashed in a heap on the ground below. The youngster was shattered. His playacting was over. No longer a boy doing a man's job—alongside men older and stronger than himself—his cockiness was destroyed.

Junior recovered the pile of potatoes and the hand truck after a good deal of derision by the crew and he made several more trips back and forth between the grader and the railroad car. But he had neither the stomach nor the muscles to finish the day. The quarter-ton load was too much for him and he finally gave it all up in despair. The question was, what would he do for money until he got a new job? It was Tuesday and he had more than twenty hours at $1.00 an hour logged on Mr. Tony's fiber clipboard. Would the bossman give him his wages even though payday wasn't until Saturday?

Mr. Tony furnished the answer very quickly:

"You been dogging it all day long, boy. I seen you makin' all them trips to the john. We don't pay around here 'till Saturday! You know that! Now you can get off the place and don't come back 'till payday! I don't want you hangin' around here getting in the way and bothering nobody."

The boy was utterly crushed at the grader boss's edict, but it wasn't until a little later, in talks with the other truckers, that the full impact of it hit me. The purpose of the order to increase the load was not only to get the railroad car loaded in a hurry, but to separate the men from the boys in the crew. It was at the same time a gimmick employers often used to make the work so tough that a man quit and moved on. It would not have been uncommon, for example, for someone like Junior to find work at another location and never return on Saturday for his pay. It would have been his contribution of free labor.

Sometimes, I learned from the grader crew, a worker will come back for his wages, after leaving in advance of payday, only to be brushed off again. The employer—and many times the migrant-crew contractor—develops a conveniently faulty memory and can't remember hiring the man; or the records have been suddenly lost; or payday has passed and they can't get enough cash—or a check drawn—right away. "Come back later, boy, and we'll see what we can do," is often the only answer a hapless employee gets from the boss and ultimately he gives it up as a total loss. There are no time clocks in the potato fields or at many of the backwoods grading establishments. The only records kept are those of the bossman and frequently he is a man—or a woman—who has had only the skimpiest education. Whatever records he maintains are for his own benefit, not for that of the hired hands. Minimum-wage laws simply don't apply at many mechanical agricultural operations, and there are no limitations on the number of hours of work. There is no grievance machinery through which the help can seek redress of maltreatment. The bossman represents the only labor relations there are and you do exactly what he says to do until he says you can stop. Cheating is frequently flagrant; exploitation is crude; protection against chicanery and deception is virtually nonexistent. "Market prices are down," a hired hand is sometimes told when he is shortchanged on payday. Often it's, "I forgot to tell you you're working for 80 cents an hour, not the dollar an hour you thought." Even more crudely, it can go, "My books don't show nothing like the hours you said you worked." And many a migrant farm worker has had the field boss or crew leader tell him, "I can't find your name in my records nowhere. You must have hired on with some other crew."

And the worker has no say in determining the conditions under which he labors. He takes a job wherever he finds it, under rules the bossman prescribes. There are few shop stewards, almost no business agents, in the fields or processing establishments, particularly in small towns and out-of-the-way farm hamlets. Contracts between employer and employee are notoriously rare. As a matter of fact, labor-management relations in terms of regulation of working hours, wages, working conditions and other benefits is a concept to which the overwhelming majority of migrant workers have never been exposed. The only grievance machinery they know about is to raise hell with the bossman if they dare and hope they are not fired on the spot, or still worse, clubbed "up 'side the head" with a fist or a stick.

The transient harvester has for the most part been left completely out of the organized-labor community. Feeble, abortive attempts have been made to establish farm-labor locals in the Far West and Southwest. There has been almost no activity in this direction in the East. The Agricultural Workers Organizing Committee has sought to strengthen and solidify its few scattered locals in California in the past few years. In Louisiana, the Agricultural and Allied Workers Union made some progress in 1962 and 1963, by obtaining recognition to represent several hundred persons employed in horse-racing, cattle, and poultry operations. The over-all efforts of labor leadership to bring farm workers under the umbrella of union protection can only be described as ineffectual. The reasons for this are not difficult to pinpoint. The itinerant harvester is for the most part unread, unskilled, and unsophisticated in the nuances of mid-twentieth-century labor relations. He is unorganized and inarticulate. He has been purposely, specifically written out of the broad body of protective legislative and administrative safeguards which protect the rights and safety of the factory worker. He is in the isolation ward of the American labor picture. His earnings are so minute that he could make virtually no contribution to labor-union coffers. He could not carry his share of organization expenses. Not the least of the barriers to his membership in organized labor is that the transiency of the seasonal interstate farm worker together with the short work periods, for many different employers, simply compounds the futility of efforts to establish stable, permanent union locals or regional farm-labor councils. While his role in the harvest of foodstuffs is essential, he remains completely apart from every other arm of the trade-union movement.

I was bone-weary when I limped away from Mr. Tony's grading and packing shed. What I wanted more than anything else was a place to rest my aching body. The labor had not been nearly as taxing as stooping over and crawling through the rows in the Homestead tomato field, but as a hand trucker I had called upon muscles that hadn't been used in a long time. Eleven hours of hustling the truck along the board platform and up the ramp into boxcars had intensified the soreness of several days before. But I learned quickly that a room with a bath was not to be had in the little town. The colored part of the hamlet lay just across the Atlantic Coast Line tracks from Norton's grader and I found there the only accommodation available. It was a seedy, dirty, 10-by-12-foot cubicle in a rooming house, for $5.00 a week or $1.50 a day.

The sun of many summers had burned the building's

wood siding a dingy brown. Two-thirds of the porch roof had weathered and rotted away. The remaining portion hung precariously, dangerously, to the right as you faced it from the dirt street. Two windows in the front of the building, at either side of the front door, were covered with the bottoms of cardboard packing cartons, so that there was no view of the interior. Jagged fragments of window glass hung in the frames, but there wasn't enough glass in either of the windows to afford any protection from the elements, or to permit any light to penetrate inside.

Rows of tiny rooms, each with its own door, opened off both sides of a narrow corridor. There were six rooms on the left side and five on the right. Halfway down the right side of the hallway was a kitchen. It was shared by all of the tenants whose misfortune it was to reside in the rooming house. The kitchen was equipped with a four-burner kerosene stove which had been blackened and grease-encrusted during the preparation of many skillets of bacon and fried chicken.

The stove worked well enough, when the landlord—or the tenants—supplied kerosene, but the thought of cooking a meal on it conjured up utter stomach-turning nausea.

An inch-thick layer of greasy water covered the bottom of the kitchen sink. Some of the tenants had poured renderings from the frying pans into the bowl after cooking a meal; it had clogged up the drain.

There was a scarred, burnt, porcelain-top table in the kitchen, but there were no chairs. Nor was there a refrigerator in which to keep milk or vegetables.

These were the cooking facilities for all of the eighteen tenants who resided in Baker's rooming house—$5.00 a week or $1.50 a night. It was a place only for those who were hardy and courageous enough to tolerate the malodorous filth; those who were agile enough to fight off the flies and roaches; those who were quick enough to get to their dinner before the vermin.

It was the seasonal residence of James E. Jackson and his wife, Ethel, and their two-month-old son, Abraham.

The Jacksons had arrived in the town on a crew bus

early during the potato season for the plowing and planting. It was their third consecutive visit there. They would remain until the last load was trucked in from the fields and washed and packed at the grading shed for shipment to market.

James Jackson was a short, squat, very black man about twenty-five. He had been born on a sharecropper farm somewhere near Clarksdale, Mississippi. He talked little and when he did it was only in guttural, almost unintelligible grunts and snorts. If he answered, "Fine!" or "Okay!" to a "How-do-you-do?" it was for him a lengthy, involved conversation.

His schooling had been interrupted—temporarily—at the age of seven for work in the cotton patches near Clarksdale. That temporary absence from a one-room country classroom extended into the eighteenth year.

For James Jackson, farm labor, on the season, at hundreds of nameless, indistinguishable wide places along various highways—both north and south—and collecting his meager pay at the end of the week was the sum total of his existence. That was his only dimension. He knew nothing of what lay beyond the horizon of a vegetable field.

Ethel Jackson was much like her husband. She was a long-suffering, taciturn woman who accepted with resignation, without complaint, the crudities and hardships imposed upon her by her station in life as a migratory agricultural worker. That was the way it was on the season; that was the role that had been assigned to her and she had neither choice nor control.

My introduction to Abraham, in the middle of an oppressively hot, stiflingly humid Saturday night, was a piercing shriek which shattered the night's stillness. I sprang up, fully clothed, in my cubicle next door to the Jacksons'. I had gone to bed in my shirt and trousers, first, because the one dollar and fifty cents I had paid for the only night's lodging I had been able to find did not include blankets and sheets, and second, because I had no idea what might take place in the night which could require my immediate exit.

There was no lock on the door which closed my room off

from the narrow corridor, so I had propped a broken-backed chair against it to insure at least minimal privacy.

The cries next door sounded desperate, urgent, as I got out of bed and went to investigate. The door to the Jackson abode was ajar and while I fumbled around for a light switch, Abraham continued to wail. When the naked bulb threw its faint light into the shadows, it became graphically, frighteningly clear why the infant was in terror: a column of large, beetlelike insects was marching, like a platoon of infantrymen in single file, across his night clothes and over his brown face. One of the insects had crawled into the child's nostril and the little fellow was flailing aimlessly with both hands in his efforts to fight off the invaders. Here was instinctive self-preservation at its rawest.

I brushed the bugs away from the child's face and ground them into the floor with my stocking feet. Then I sat quietly beside him until his mother returned. Believing that he was safely, soundly asleep in the cardboard cabbage carton which served as his crib, Ethel Jackson had sought an evening's diversion at the lone colored tavern in town. It was payday and her husband was elsewhere. She didn't know where. But the woman had drudged ten hours a day for six days, inspecting and grading potatoes, and the tavern offered the only recreation available for migrants.

She had tucked a bleached, freshly laundered burlap potato sack around her son in his cardboard crib before she went out and left him—she thought—safely asleep.

She rushed to the child as soon as she walked into the room. I explained my presence and she took her infant son up in her arms.

"Them bugs is everywhere," she declared. "They're in the fields, in the food, in the bed, everywhere. Ain't no place you can get away from them." She shuddered, and on her face was the look of utter defeat. "What can you do? We got to live someplace. Jus' ain' noplace else for us folks comes here on the season."

Ethel was a young woman, in her early twenties,

perhaps. Yet despite her youth, despite her girlish figure and the trim, pointed breasts which strained for escape from her summer blouse, her face was that of a woman who had lived the hard life; a woman who had lived with suffering and pain and knew about doing without.

Her legs and thighs were slim and well formed. The tiny waist was in perfect proportion to the rest of her figure. Even without grooming, even in the absence of appropriate attire, she was startlingly attractive—the large, warm, brown eyes; the smooth complexion; the full lips and bright even teeth.

In the closeness of his mother's arms the child forgot the terror caused by the insects marching across his face. He nestled against the firm breasts and gurgled contentedly.

The chair Ethel sat in had a high back and cane bottom. She had thanked me graciously after she finished making the infant comfortable and said she guessed her husband would be home soon. It had been payday for him, too. She sat spread-legged in the chair, rocking the child gently, and the weariness I had seen moments earlier on her face, the defeat that had covered her features like a mask, gave way to contentment in the inexplicable bond that exists only between a mother and her child.

The infant, Ethel Jackson volunteered matter-of-factly, had been born there in that room in Baker's rooming house, under the dim naked light that hung overhead.

"It was Sunday night," she recalled. "The pains started right quick and there wasn't nobody here but James. There wasn't no time to get a doctor. Didn't know where to find one. My husband did what had to be done. I watched him and told him what to do. The doctor—he came sometime later—said James did a wonderful job, too."

Ethel had returned to her 60-cents-hourly job at the grading shed across the railroad tracks a few days after giving birth to her child.

"I had to go back," she declared, "or somebody else would have got my job. With Abraham here we needed the money more than before."

A few days of work at Mr. Tony's grading and packing shed, and to bed in exhaustion at night with my clothes on in my $1.50 closet in the run-down rooming house was for me enough exposure to the upstate Florida potato country. I did not find it necessary to brush any more insects out of the Jackson infant's nostrils, so I gathered up my few belongings, packed them in my shopping-bag carrier and caught the first available Greyhound bus headed north—this time to Charleston, South Carolina. The old Confederate city is a major junction for the easternmost stream of migratory agricultural workers journeying northward from Florida's lush, green fruit and vegetable fields, along the Atlantic Seaboard to the harvest in Virginia, Maryland, Delaware, and New Jersey—then on to New York and New England.

During the season, from roughly early May to late September, the catfish and cornbread seaport, still a bastion of the Old South, is a bubbling, seething, teeming mélange of humanity. Giant over-the-road trailer trucks stream into and out of the city at all hours, heavily freighted with cargoes of every description. There is furious activity around the clock, at the produce markets as men hand-truck incoming crates, baskets, and boxes of foodstuffs out of the trailer vans and railroad cars, then reload it in other conveyances for transshipment.

Battered old buses, long retired from service as transporters of school children, lumber into the city over every highway, loaded with crop pickers on their way up the road. Many farm-labor crews arrive and depart on the backs of trucks, some of them seated on pine benches, others sprawled across assorted harvest gear for the long haul. Still others find resting places on the journey wherever they can.

The comings and goings of the itinerant, interstate harvesters I observed in Charleston were virtually exact duplications of travel conditions so poignantly reported by A. E. Farrell in *Good Housekeeping* magazine in November of 1960:

> The squalor . . . is readily apparent when life is viewed first hand. Let us follow a crew as it leaves its home

> base in Belle Glade, Florida, on its annual trek north in search of work. Loaded like cattle on the back of a truck, the children and their parents are jammed in with foot lockers, cardboard boxes, oilstoves, rusty bedsprings, wash-tubs and other paraphernalia. The crew leaves Belle Glade at 8:45 P.M. At 11 it stops for a meal in Fort Pierce, Florida, but is told by the owner of the diner to move on. At 1:10 it stops in Melbourne, Florida, for gas, but crew members are not permitted to use toilets. At 1:55 A.M., there is a "bathroom" stop in the woods. At 6:20 A.M. the truck stops at a country store outside Daytona Beach for "breakfast." The children are fed bread, soft drinks and a few cold cuts. At 12:00 noon another stop is made for water at a spring. The water turns out to be polluted with sulphur. State troopers follow the truck through many towns (to be sure nobody disembarks). At 8:00 P.M. another stop at Bay Harbour, South Carolina. State troopers make the crew remain on the truck during the stop. At 11 A.M. the following morning (14 hours after departing Belle Glade) the crew finally arrives at the grower's camp.

Farrell's account was similar in many respects to that of my own trip from Homestead to the labor camp which the grower had abandoned in west central Florida, and his description of children traveling along with their parents was a replay of my own experiences with little Virginia Lee:

> Everywhere the migrants were unwelcome strangers, eyed suspiciously by residents and police. For children the trip was unusually wearing. They arrive dirty, cranky and tired. No wonder one ten-year-old complained wistfully to me, "I don't like travelin'. When I gets sleepy I can't sleep. Too much noise and not enough room. Don't get enough to eat. No milk . . ."

Many of the migrant crews rumble into Charleston in old vehicles from much farther away than Belle Glade—from Georgia, Alabama, Louisiana, even as far away as Mississippi and Texas. A great number of the open trucks and broken-down buses and passenger cars used to haul migrants are badly in need of repairs. A spot check of several hundred vehicles in New Jersey in the late summer of 1963 revealed, for example, that more than half of them should have been ordered out of service and junked. An inspector recalled that a bus loaded for the return trip from New Jersey to Florida in November, 1963, was found to have been operating with one rear wheel fastened to its drum by a single bolt. Accidents causing serious injuries and fatalities are not uncommon. Motor-vehicle-inspection laws are not applied in the transportation of migrants as they are for others—for the transportation of livestock, for example. The States of California, Colorado, Connecticut, New York, Oregon, Pennsylvania, West Virginia, and North Carolina have laws and regulations setting safety standards of one kind or another for vehicles used in moving farm help, but most are entirely inadequate and largely unenforced.

Under a federal law, the Interstate Commerce Commission is authorized to establish regulations setting minimum standards for the safety and comfort of migrant farm workers on the move, but only for carriers which travel a total distance of seventy-five miles and across state lines. Requirements under this law state that vehicle operators must be twenty-one years of age or more and that meal stops be made at least every six hours; that rest stops be made, and that passengers be protected from rain and cold. The ICC also specifics certain minimum requirements for vehicle equipment. The grim fact is, however, that the Commission employs approximately 135 vehicle inspectors, on a nation-wide basis, and many, many crew leaders with their weary, hungry, road-tired loads of harvesters are never halted at ICC checkpoints.

5

The Migrant's a Dreamer

A grandiose dream of the interstate migratory agricultural worker, born and reared in a tar-paper shanty in the backwoods Deep South, is that his first trip up the road, 'way up north, on the season, will be his last. He has heard tell, perhaps from friends or relatives who've made the trip—or trips—before, maybe from a fellow stoop laborer with whom he worked side by side in a bean patch, that he'll find a pot of gold at the end of his rainbow and there'll be no bossman to take his share off the top. He's heard, too, that everybody lives big "up north" where the big cities are and that "they" don't allow cheating on wages. He's been told that he would get paid for every hour he worked up the road in the north—

sometimes even at overtime rates. The "gov'mint" takes care of everyone who needs help, as long as they need it, but most of the time you can make it easily enough on your own.

There was a period of relative calm in the migrant stream during my travels with itinerant harvesters as far as Charleston. The truck crops in the heavily agricultural Charleston Harbor area—John's Island, Young's Island, Wadmalow Island, and the surrounding towns of Edisto and Hollywood—had not reached peak maturity. The inflow of field help was far greater than the demand. There was a heavy surplus in the labor supply. I decided at that point to follow the migrant's dream and find out for myself what lay at the end of his rainbow.

I found quickly, while working and living and traveling in Delaware and New Jersey, that the South has no corner on misery; Florida, Georgia, and the Carolinas have no monopoly on despair.

You turn off the highway that leads into a village in southern New Jersey, just before approaching the center of town. You walk a short distance, half a mile perhaps, along a blacktop road. There, on the right, tucked away in a cluster of maples, you will find Mrs. Hazel Watkins' camp.

It is a tiny enclave of tortured earth, adjoining broad, luxuriant acres of salad-bowl vegetables, only minutes away from the town crossroads. You are confronted with the shocking reality that after the migrant suffers with his family the agony of many hours and many miles on the trip to the promised land, the conditions he finds are just as bad, if not worse, than those he left behind. Life up the road, on the season, is a nightmare, not a dream. Living conditions are just as mean as they were in the tar-paper hovel where he lived in the South; and more shattering than anything else he faces is the fact that the crew leader and bossman will cheat and exploit him just as surely, and as crudely, as if he had remained back at home.

Mrs. Watkins' camp was a shabby, neglected patch of earth that might have been lifted *en toto* out of Anywhere, Georgia, and transplanted intact many hundreds of miles to the north. All the wretchedness, all the squalor, all the ugliness of the red-hilled mule-and-plow country remained. The miserable, impoverished band of laborers that Mrs. Watkins had hauled into southern New Jersey from the snap-bean and tomato fields around Lake Okeechobee near the Florida Everglades were housed in falling-down red-shingle shanties, the likes of which I hadn't seen since Belle Glade. Mrs. Watkins had brought her workers there in an old bus and a vintage Plymouth sedan, both of which were drawn up, flat-tired on all fours, in the narrow dirt pathway that led off the blacktop feeder road. The row of shanties seemed on the verge of collapsing any minute into a heap of stinking refuse. Only a few nails held them up. They had all deteriorated to varying degrees under the relentless punishment of the weather, but the major contributors to their condition were old age and neglect.

Only the rooftops of the camp could be seen from the roadway. There was no other access to the front of the compound, since the two old vehicles sat in the way. Weeds and grass had grown up around the flat tires. It was obvious that they hadn't been—or couldn't be—moved. Mrs. Watkins' farm-labor camp was a short stretch of Tobacco Road in grim detail: the vile outdoor privy, a kerosene stove in a community kitchen, a naked water pump, rising out of the dust before one of the shanties, dripping its waste into a stagnant pool. Flies and mosquitoes buzzed hungrily about the place, and garbage and other litter were scattered all around. A knee-high barbed-wire fence surrounded the camp, where a flock of dusty chickens clucked and scratched in the debris around and under the shanties. The structures were elevated a foot or so off the ground, either to let rain water run underneath or to provide a convenient place to throw garbage. At the extreme right end of the row there were two additional reasons for the fence. A pair of mangy goats grazed in the weeds at the end of a tether, seeking whatever nourishment they could root out of the dirt. Intermingled with the smell of chickens, goats, garbage, and decay was the offensive odor of human waste. The old outhouse, on the far side of the goat yard, was tipped askew. Its door hung ajar. It was not being used at the time of my visit. The unmistakable rankness of rotted food mixed with the other odors hung over the camp in a shroud of foul stench.

Mrs. Watkins stood in the doorway of one of the cabins. She was a tall, angular woman. Her face was blank, expressionless, suggesting that she had only a moment earlier awakened from a fitful sleep to discover that nothing had changed around the place since she laid down for a nap; that the troubles she had gone to bed to forget had mutliplied in the interim both in numbers and in magnitude. Her gold-jacketed dentures flashed brightly in the shadowy gloom of the doorway. She peered—inquisitively, distrustfully—at the strange face before her in the yard in front of the cabin. Over her hair, Mrs. Watkins wore a flowered kerchief which she had tied at the back of her neck. She wore a ten-cent-store simulated-pearl necklace and a large costume-jewelry medallion dangled below between the mounds of her breasts. As she stood there, half in and half out of the gloomy cabin interior, the necklace was no more incongruous with her general appearance than the forest green whipcord lady's riding pants and the several-sizes-too-large man's shirt. She had gathered the tail in the front and tied it over her stomach. A pair of dirty tennis shoes completed her attire and holes had been cut in the toes apparently to provide ease for corns on the toes of both feet.

"Mister, I got the miseries," she replied when I inquired concerning her health. "I wish I could lay down and die right here, but I can't. I owe too many debts to die and I got all these people hangin' round here, depending on me to stay alive."

Riding pants and sneakers notwithstanding, Mrs. Watkins was a migrant-farm-labor crew leader. She had hauled the scrubby collection of workers into her camp from various little farm villages around Lake Okeechobee. She said she had wanted plenty of help on hand for the early plowing and planting, but the crops in southern New Jersey were late in the growing and there wasn't much for anyone to do. "Been here since April," she declared sorrowfully, "an' ain't a one of us made hardly enough money to buy bread. I was broke when I got here. Be the same way when I leave. Been carryin' these folks, all seventeen of them, out of my own pocket since I came up here and it don' look like I'll ever get out of the hole."

There were twenty-eight on the bus and in the old Plymouth when they left Florida. "Some of them jus' up and quit me," she said, "after I hauled 'em all the way up here and gave 'em somethin' to eat on the way. Two or three boys said they wanted to work. They wasn't lookin' for nothin' but a free ride. Last thing I knew is they got off somewhere down the road when we stopped for gas an' I ain't seen 'em since. Somebody said they was going to Philadelphia.

"Then there was my driver," she added. "He quit me just back here the other day. Now I took care of that man out of my own pocket for three or four weeks. Was goin' to pay him a dollar an hour soon's we get some work to 'mount to something. What did he do? Well, he took the money I gave him to buy gas and I ain't seen him since. If folks keep on leaving me, I won't have hardly a soul to get my contract work done when it's ready."

Mrs. Watkins resisted pressing questions. Puzzled suspicion crossed her brown face. Recent experiences had done nothing to strengthen her confidence in males of any age and her manner and speech showed it clearly. She frowned. "You must be from the gov'ment. "Askin' all them questions. You an inspector or something? The gov'ment people comes around here all the time lookin' around and writing things in their books. I don't want to be bothered. You one of them people from the State that wants to know how my help is gittin' along?"

Assurances that the stranger standing in front of her cabin in the yard was not from the government were profuse. He was just another hand looking for work and traveling up the road, on the season. She relaxed a bit, with visible reluctance and some misgivings. Her wariness in the light of the recent desertions of the strongest backs in her crew was understandable. Further, as a labor-crew contractor she had often been subjected to official scrutiny. Until the disappearance of her driver, he had dealt with officialdom in her behalf. He had presented the appropriate credentials to state troopers and to police and other authorities when necessary on the trip up the road; he had answered inquiries at check stations on the highway, where migrating crews were inspected and counted.

The tall woman was a migrant farm-labor crew leader by inheritance. A dozen years earlier she and her husband, Leroy, had purchased from a grower the row of six broken shanties and the few scraggly acres upon which they stood. They had become more or less permanent residents each season. The two of them had gathered labor crews together in the swamp country in Okeechobee County and hauled them north to New Jersey each spring, returning home at harvest's end late each fall. Some seasons, she said, they had done well. They had been able to buy the old bus on the installment plan and they had a more modern family sedan parked in the driveway back at home. But a crippling diabetic seizure had immobilized Leroy Watkins during the previous winter's slack period and it had fallen upon Hazel to carry on in his place. It was a little too early to speculate on whether or not she would be equal to the responsibility, but the evidence seemed to point to the contrary. The backbone of her crew had abandoned her and with crops already weeks late, she was spending from her reserve fund. The illness which had bedded her husband in Florida could not have occurred at a more unfortunate time.

"I got to do the best I know how," she declared, " 'till my daddy gets better. He said he might be able to come up here later on, but there jus' ain't no tellin'. He can't hardly get out of that bed. Maybe when the weather gets better and the medicine he's taking starts to work, he can drive up here and take charge of things. Then again, maybe by that time it'll be too late. I got these folks here to take care of," she declared, waving a hand over the camp around her, "an' they ain't earnin' a dime. I ain't made nothin' neither."

The chickens clucked and scratched in the dust under Mrs. Watkins' cabin as she spoke and the goats rooted and snorted in their enclosure. A man of about fifty straddled a wood bench down the line beside the door of his shanty, peeling potatoes. He dropped a pile of skins on the boardwalk under his feet and threw them by the handful to the goats. The two beasts constituted Mrs. Watkins' built-in garbage-disposal units, but they hadn't done their work well. There was enough refuse and debris scattered around the camp to feed a whole herd.

"The dirt farmer I contracts with sent for me and the crew in a hurry," she said, "and we rushed up here right away. Soon as we got here the weather went bad and we been stuck ever since. The farmer, he can't help me none. He's got problems hisself."

Spring's late arrival, she explained, coupled with a depressed market for truck crops had imposed an economic strain on the southern New Jersey produce area and the pinch was being felt all the way up the line, from the laborers who picked the vegetables to the retailers who sold them for table use. "The farmer told me when he called on the telephone that the contract would be ten cents a basket for tomatoes. He couldn' get his price at the market for what few he had in the fields, so he cut me down to eight cents for the couple of acres that was ready and Lord knows we can't make it on that."

The beleaguered lady, sensing that she had at last found a sympathetic ear into which she could pour her woes, continued, on, and on, and on. ". . . It cost me mos' two hundred dollars to bring all these folks up here," she wailed. "Then the best of them quit. There was money for gas and oil to pay an' that old bus broke down aroun' Norfolk. There was parts to pay for and then the man charged me an arm and a leg to put 'em in. Besides that, I paid that driver I had twenty-five dollars and he up and left an' took some money that I give him to buy gas. I knowed he was a thief when I laid eyes on him down there in Florida, but I had to have somebody in a hurry to drive that old bus. I couldn' do it m'self."

Mrs. Watkins unfolded her arms from across her chest and slumped into a chair outside her door. She extended her feet and legs out before her, rested one elbow on her knee, cupped her chin with the right hand, and moaned wearily, "I'm a woman who got the blues. I can't see no way clear. I tell you the truth, Mister, I wish I could lay down and die. But I can't leave my man back home in Florida; an' I owes too many people to go anywhere now."

The prior owner of the site where the camp stood had permitted the place to fall apart and the Watkinses hadn't done very much to improve conditions. The single row of six one-story tar-paper shanties faced a dirt pathway which had been rutted and scarred over the years by frequent foot traffic. A few two-by-eight planks had been thrown over pools of rain and drain water that collected in the low spots.

In the cabin next to the woman crew leader's I found Mr. Willie. The old man's shanty, like the other structures in the row, had no basement. Garbage and other refuse had collected in the air space underneath. It was midafternoon of a summer day and slivers of light showed through the cracks and rents in the roof overhead. Here and there he had placed containers to catch the rainwater that always dripped in during a storm—a dishpan in the corner, where the once-whitewashed walls had been stained an ugly rust-brown by the rains streaming in between the joints; a galvanized scrub pail at the foot of the bed where the roofing had been torn loose by a strong wind.

Mr. Willie was an old man, gnarled and stoop-shouldered. The few teeth that remained in the front of his mouth were stained a deep brown by the cud of snuff he carried almost perpetually under his lower lip. He had been dipping it for a good many years and he moved the wad expertly around in his mouth with the tip of his tongue, the better to extract the last bit of flavor, the better to savor the last bit of juice.

He spent much of his time sitting on the edge of his rusty cot—thinking, contemplating his lot, the hard life he had spent in the fields. There wasn't much work to do since the weather had put the growing behind; besides Mr. Willie couldn't work very fast, not nearly as fast as the younger men—or even the women—in the crew. He picked a few baskets of tomatoes in the morning hours, when there were tomato patches ready to work in, then he plodded on back to his little shack. It bothered him a little bit that he couldn't work as long and as hard as the rest of the crew. There had been times in his long past when he had done five times as much work as anyone else had, and then after finishing up at the end of the day, he had raised hell with the women at night.

Nowadays it took Mr. Willie a long time to crawl through the rows and he got tired in the hot sun. It took him a long time even to come home for he walked slowly, a little painfully, because of the aches in his joints. Sometimes when he went up the three steps that led into his shanty, he would steady himself by grasping the doorframe before he put the first foot inside. Even when he was hungry after a few hours in the field, he would sit on the edge of his cot until he regained enough strength to get up and throw something together—a can of soup, or some baked beans, or something.

Mr. Willie lived alone in the cabin. There was no one to do for him. There was no one anywhere that he could look to for help when he needed it. He was a widower and his sons and daughters had grown up and scattered. He had long ago lost all contact with them. Leroy and Hazel Watkins were really the only "family" he had.

The furnishings in Mr. Willie's abode were meager. The iron cot around which most of his life revolved was just long enough and wide enough for his small frame. It was simply constructed of L-angle iron strips strung with a mesh spring. A tattered old quilt covered the cotton mattress on the cot, which was pushed flush up against one wall. The rain that had so often leaked into the tar-paper shanty had stained the pine flooring as well as the whitewashed walls. The biggest holes in the ceiling had only recently developed and Mrs. Watkins hadn't had a chance to have them fixed. The old man didn't complain, though. He knew all about the bad things that were happening to her, and to her husband, Leroy, back home in Florida.

The other articles of furniture in Mr. Willie's place consisted of a metal olive-drab portable closet with batwing doors, a chest of drawers, a small table, and two camp stools. One of the doors to the closet was open and I could see hanging inside a gray pin-striped suit coat, a pair of trousers to match, and on the floor a pair of worn, high-top black shoes. A white shirt also hung in the closet, as though it had been worn a few times and hung there to be used again before laundering. What had once been a fancy mirror, with a heavy wood-carved frame, was mounted over the chest of drawers. On the chest were the old man's personal belongings: a comb, a brush—though he didn't have very much hair—a safety razor, and three or four bottles of assorted patent medicines for his aches and pains. The items were arranged neatly in a line on top of the chest.

Mr. Willie sat cross-legged on the edge of his cot, transferring the cud of snuff back and forth from one side of his mouth to the other, and declared with careful emphasis: "Time was when I could pick and load and tote things in the fields from 'fore day in the mornin' till black dark at night. Then I'd collect my money and go look for some girl. Aw, man, I was real tough with the women. Was raised aroun' Clearwater, Florida, an' all the women knew me there—till I got married. The woman he married ("She sure straightened me up!") had borne him four sons and three daughters, but she was now twenty years in her grave. A part of the old man had died with her; he never really recovered. The family had gone off to he didn't know where and he was restless, footloose, like a gypsy. Moving from one place to another with any old band of traveling harvesters was as near to a perfect mode of living as he would ever achieve. He didn't own anything. He didn't want to. He had no real responsibilities, except to himself. He needed cash occasionally to buy the necessary medicaments at the drugstore to ease the pains that came along with the advancing years; he needed a new white shirt now and then, and a pair of socks or two, and some underwear. But he could earn enough money for these necessities by picking a few baskets of tomatoes when he felt like it, or pulling four or five hampers of beans. When the season went down in South Jersey, he would climb back on Mrs. Watkins' bus, one step at a time and ride back to Clearwater, where it was warm; where he knew folks and folks knew him.

He clasped his hands over a knee, leaned back a little bit on the edge of the cot and observed, "Can't do much field work any more. Gettin' old. Gettin' tired. Ain't up to it like I used to be. Ain't necessary to do that hard work no more. I jus' work a little bit in the mornings before the sun gets too hot, then I come back here to my place, and sit around and take it easy till the rest of the folks come in. Miz Watkins ain' doin' so good this season, but it don't bother me. I wasn't fixin' to raise no sweat when I come up here, an' I feels a little sorry for her. No man on the place to help her look out for things an' Leroy sick in his bed down there at home."

That was retirement for Mr. Willie, traveling along with the migrant workers when he felt like it and doing just a little bit of work until he got tired. Social Security and Old Age Assistance benefits were abstractions that didn't exist in his lexicon. No one had told him that there were provisions for taking care of the aged. He hadn't asked. He didn't know. What he had known for nearly seventy years—all of his life—was hard labor. When he contemplated the role he had played in three score and ten years it extended no further than a hard day's work in the fields, on the season, collecting his money and going out to raise hell. There was nothing else, really, for him to consider. That had been his life and what else was there before him now except to return to Clearwater when the time came, then perhaps back to South Jersey again with Mrs. Watkins the next spring?

"Been comin' up here off an' on a whole gang of years," he said, "most of the time with Leroy and Hazel. This year's the worst, but I ain' bothered. Too old now to worry about that. Was choppin' lettuce for a grower a couple days back, jus' to keep busy till the tomatoes came in. The bossman said he was payin' a dollar an hour when we started. Time came to line up for our money he didn' give us but eighty-five cents. I guess he disremembered he was short on the hour. That didn' bother me neither. Ain' nothing you can do. The money's all folded up in a envelope when he gits to you in the line, so you jus' takes what the bossman gives you and you gits out of the way for somebody else . . ."

I met Hermano Alvarez at the bus station in the South Jersey town when I left Mrs. Watkins' camp in the clearing behind the cluster of maples and walked back down the black-top road. Hermano was a husky six-footer in his mid-twenties. He chain-smoked Pall Mall cigarettes as I watched him hunched over on the hard bench. He was a portrait of despair. He spoke little English, having arrived on his first visit to the States from Ponce, Puerto Rico, only two months earlier. My own Spanish was scarcely rudimentary, but after a period of linguistic experimentation this message came through:

"The Seabrook Farms people here in Bridgeton they pay pretty good. I worked there as a laborer for a dollar and a quarter an hour. I had a little money when I came here, so I told them to keep my wages on the books. I didn't want to carry it around. When I was ready to draw my money, the paymaster gave me one hundred and eighty-six dollars. It was enough to send home to my wife and children in Ponce. After I cashed the check at the bank, I didn't know where the Post Office was, so I went into a bar to ask. Maybe somebody saw the money; I don't remember. But there was a girl at the bar and I bought her a drink and I had a couple of beers for my-self. Then I don't remember anything else, except going out of the bar with the girl and we walked up some stairs.

"When I woke up all the money was gone. The girl was gone, too.

"Only two bottles of beer, but they tasted very funny. . . . The bartender, he knew the girl. She was going to show me the Post Office, but we went up two flights of stairs . . ."

Hermano's story was repeated in various forms many times over in Bridgeton and in similar farm-industry centers along the Atlantic Seaboard. Women with an eye for the easy, fast buck descend on Bridgeton and places like it as regularly as payday arrives. They come from Philadelphia, Camden, Atlantic City, and Asbury Park, where they have learned with superior skill the trick of separating a farm or food-process-plant worker from his wages.

A woman I met in a Bridgeton tavern said she had only recently arrived from South Carolina with a migrant crew and that she faced a major crisis.

"My baby is sick with pneumonia at home," she wept, "and I need money right away for medicine. I'll go to bed with you if you 'loan' me ten dollars. I'll pay it back out of my first paycheck." Later I learned that she was one of a string of girls who had loose working arrangements with a taxicab driver. He furnished transportation and rooms by the hour; the girls paid him a fixed fee per client.

The midseason working population multiplies in Bridgeton and similar agricultural towns. Big-city operators have long ago learned to take advantage of paydays. One Atlantic City sharpie made regular Friday-to-Sunday visits to Bridgeton, with three girls in a closed pickup van. The vehicle was equipped with a folding cot in the back and it could be driven around town from place to place wherever business was best. The price per visit varied from $10 to $20, depending on the client's anxiety and the sales ability of the girls.

The entrepreneur, with his mobile whorehouse, worked a regular circuit in south central New Jersey, visiting various towns at times carefully planned to coincide with paydays. It was a risky, uncertain racket, but expenses were minimal and profits high. In a way, he was a migrant-crew leader, too, but not of farm laborers; his crew members' services were performed in the van, not the fields.

On the side the Atlantic City man trafficked in after-hours liquor by the drink or the bottle, and as a traveling salesman, he undoubtedly did well.

Ernest Parnell was a big, homely, bespectacled man who after twenty-five years of working the fields, on the season, had at last achieved a degree of status: He was a migrant-crew leader. His winter headquarters were in Clewiston, Florida, alongside Lake Okeechobee, but from April to October he could be found, with his crew, harvesting tomatoes and snap beans and potatoes in Central New Jersey until there were no more crops to pick.

He was basically an honest man and he dealt with his crew—and with growers for whom he contracted—as though every other man was honest, too. At times Ernest's honesty worked against him, for he was unaware that he was being taken advantage of.

He owned two buses, two flatbed trucks, and a pickup truck in which he had hauled his laborers into central New Jersey from Clewiston. The camp they occupied was in a tree-shaded hollow near Cowtown. It was, as usual, out of sight of the main road.

The members of Ernest's crew were all Negroes. Some had worked with him for three or four years. There was a combination truck driver-mechanic who also acted as Ernest's next in command. He could neither read nor write his own name, but he could diagnose and correct the many imperfections of the ancient gasoline engines which powered the crew boss's vehicles and he was therefore a valuable man to have around.

"Did you say," Ernest asked me, scratching his head, "that there's some Puerto Rican hands working the same fields for the same grower and gettin' more piece-work pay than my crew?"

Assured that this was the truth on the evidence of pay-check stubs I had examined, thc big man crawled back under the hood of the truck on which he was working and mumbled, "Got to see about that."

It was indeed the truth, but the chance that Parnell would make anything of it was remote. There was no reason for him not to believe the grower with whom he had made a verbal contract. After all, hadn't he picked out this bossman's fields for a good many years on nothing more than a word-of-mouth agreement; and hadn't the boss paid him every dime he was owed?

The fact was that Parnell had contracted with the grower to put his crew of 40 men and women to work harvesting tomatoes for 10 cents a basket, while a group of Puerto Rican workers under government contract were picking adjoining fields owned by the same grower for 12 to 14 cents. The pay differential amounted to $1.50 to $2.00 less per day for the men—and a few women—in Parnell's crew. He and his gang were paying a color tax that they didn't know existed.

The grower used other gimmicks to limit the earnings of Parnell's group. Before the pickers begin their work in the mornings, the grower's truck drives into the fields with hundreds upon hundreds of five-eighths-of-a-bushel baskets. Often the basket supply runs out by midday. With no baskets to fill, the day's work ends. Yet, at the same time, in adjoining fields owned by the same grower, Puerto Rican harvesters have an oversupply of baskets and they pick until sundown.

The practice had the effect of guaranteeing an oversupply of labor which could be paid the lowest piece rate while laborers in neighboring fields were paid more. It was outrageously crude exploitation of crew and crew leader, which Parnell seemed to know nothing about. He accepted the fact that the basket supply was exhausted and that work had to cease.

Freddy King, one of the 40 members of Ernest Parnell's Clewiston crew was more vocal with his sentiments:

"One morning we went into the bean fields and there was only four hundred hampers. We had twenty-five hands on the job that day and we run out of baskets in two hours. I think the big bossman figured it that way, so we wouldn't earn any money and we'd go in debt with him for food and rent. Well, goddamit, we did."

Exploitation of migrant farm workers is not by any means exclusive to growers. A large share of the guilt lies with greedy, unscrupulous crew bosses. In another field near Cowtown, I found a glaring example of how one typical abuse works.

Every morning just after sunup during the snap-bean season, a convoy of buses grinds to a halt on the roadside near a vast field operated by one of the large New Jersey growers. Men and women tumble out of the buses and rush to the head of the rows. The maximum piece rate is 40 cents for each hamper picked.

This is the "day haul" labor, brought into the central New Jersey fields from Camden, Philadelphia, Chester, and other nearby cities. They are people picked up on the street corners for work by the day. There are men and women and a few children.

If the crew leader hauls 40 workers into the fields, they can average 20 to 30 hampers of beans per day, at 40 cents for each hamper—that is, from $8 to $12 a day. If the crew leader collects 10 cents from the grower for each hamper his crew picks, his share, called the "over-ride," is $80 to $120 for the day. If he drives his own bus, his only expenses are for gasoline and oil. If the crew leader pays a driver, $15 to $20 is deducted from the grower's contracted sum for that fee. Many day-haul crew leaders operate three or four buses and their profits, even after expenses, are proportionately astronomical.

There are no deductions for Social Security or federal or state income taxes. The grower pays each crew leader a lump sum at the end of the day and he in turn pays his help. Cheating by crew leaders is the rule, not the exception, and there is neither recourse nor appeal for the victims. It is a day-to-day operation, with minimum governmental controls. Since the crew often differs from one day to the next during the season, the leader rarely has to deal with those he shortchanged in the past. They join other crews and work in other fields. There is usually an oversupply of day-haul labor, so that work in the fields is almost always an employer's market. He dictates the standards and there are no labor-management negotiations through which conditions agreeable to both are thrashed out. Work is on the employer's terms or not at all.

Thomas Miller, aged fifty-one, sat by the side of the highway near Manalapan in central New Jersey, moaning plaintively like a small child.

"Five years," he wept, mopping the tears away with a

handkerchief, "I been traveling up the road on the season with Dorothy Hall and I ain't never been treated so bad. That woman been cheatin' me out of the wages she owes me and then she been chargin' me rent to live in a place that's 'damned.' "

Miller was an unshaven bedraggled man and he appeared to be badly in need of a bath. He managed to control himself long enough to explain that crew leader Dorothy Hall had freighted a load of fifteen male and female workers into the tiny hamlet of Manalapan from Plant City, Florida, to harvest the beans and celery and potatoes. She had housed them in tumble-down shacks in a clump of trees 200 yards off the highway and charged them $7.00 weekly per person.

Miller complained that he shared living space with four men and three women, none of them related, in one of the single-room shacks at total rental of $49 a week. What Dorothy Hall had not told her migrant help was that county authorities had condemned the squatter community several months earlier and that it had been scheduled for demolition as a health hazard. It was bordered on one side by a 100-foot-square pool of foul stagnant water and on another side by a row of weather-worn privies.

The woman crew boss had been collecting rent regularly for several weeks from each of fifteen laborers in her crew on the pretense that she was taking care of the landlord. The truth was that the authorities had taken over the property, pending destruction, and Miss Hall was stuffing the rentals into her own purse.

Miller said he had earned $21 for one week of work with the Dorothy Hall crew of which $7 was due the grocer for food and another $7 for rent in the "damned" shack. His net, therefore, was $7 for seven days' labor.

"That woman robbed me," Miller declared, wiping his face with the dirty handkerchief again, "and I'm stayin' right here by the road till a state trooper comes by. Gonna have her arrested 'less she pays me the money that's due. She been chargin' rent for that old shanty that's 'damned' and puttin' the money in her own pocket. She ain't paid no landlord. There ain't none to pay."

The place where Miller resided on the season was in a double row of simulated red-brick shingled shanties facing a wide dirt roadway. There were five one-story shacks in the row on the right and seven or eight on the left. A mangy dog bothered what edible garbage there was in a shopping bag some one had left near the stoop leading into one of the shacks; another miserable mongrel, perhaps the hungry one's kin, sprawled in the shade nearby. Three or four brown, half-naked children played at hop-scotch in the dirt. They had marked off their court in the earth with a stick, and they used beer-bottle caps to show the blocks they had successfully skipped.

The sun was hot; they were all barefoot. They laughed and argued the way children do in competitive games. It was their playground, and noontime was their recreation hour.

The wreck of an old Ford sedan reposed like an unburied skeleton next to one of the shanties and the kids had been playing on and around it, too. There were tiny barefoot prints on the hood and the roof. One of their games had been warfare at sea and the sedan had served as flagship of the fleet.

The biggest boy, the one in the striped T-shirt and ragged overalls, had been the admiral. He was the loudest; he argued more than the others. The rest of the kids were the crew.

Just to the left of the entrance way leading to the camp was the community water pump. It served all of the fifty to sixty tenants who lived there. The pump was mounted on a concrete slab and before it produced more than a trickle of water it had to be hand-cranked vigorously for three or four minutes. Then the water came in a gush and splashed over a pail provided to catch the drippings, and into pools around the slab.

A little farther along the wide roadway, to the right, was a long one-story building; it, too, was covered with simulated red-brick shingles. It was the only multiple dwelling in the camp. There were three adjoining apartments under the same roof, each with its own entrance.

A screen door, fallen away from one of the entrances, leaned against the front of the house. Three brick chimneys, one for a cookstove in each unit, rose skyward from the top of the building. Smoke from wood stoves—in midsummer—vanished into the breeze from two of the chimneys.

Mrs. Isabelle Johnson, the mother of three, occupied the two-room unit in the center of the long building.

She shooed the flies away from an infant asleep in a cot and declared, "That child ain't got a chance. His daddy and me want to give him the best, but we can't do no better than this."

Mrs. Johnson had been a tenant at the camp for three years. She had moved there with her husband on her first visit to central New Jersey on the season.

"Well, it was like this," she explained. "My husband got laid off from his job at that sawmill near Essex, Virginia. There was this busload of people going through, so we got on. We heard all the talk about a lot of work in the fields in New Jersey at good wages. We didn't have nothing to lose, so we got on and came here.

"The first year wasn't so bad," the young mother related, "and we moved into this place kind of temporary. Me and my husband both worked in the tomato fields. Then when potatoes were ready, we picked up behind the digging machine. We even bought a secondhand car and George drove it back and forth to the different jobs he found. But I started having babies one right after the other and now we can't get out of this place. Can't find no landlords that take farm people with children, so we got to stay here."

Mrs. Johnson and her husband, George, paid $15 weekly rent for the two rooms they lived in. There was no bath, no indoor plumbing, and no sanitary facilities—only the community outhouse to the rear, which they shared with the rest of the tenants. The only time they knew that a landlord existed was when he sent a rent collector around on Saturday morning. The owner rarely appeared. The couple wanted desperately to return to Virginia with their children, where they would be with the rest of their families and friends, but because of the weekly rent, expenses for food and medicine and other necessities, they were unable to save enough for the trip.

"We're stranded here in this awful place," Mrs. Johnson lamented, "and there just ain't a thing we can do."

A few miles away in Hightstown, New Jersey, a wizened little man sat on the tracks on a railroad siding in the heart of the Negro section of town, contemplating an agonizing dilemma: he didn't know where his next meal or his next bottle of wine were coming from. Hunched over, his knees doubled up in a knot, he was a rare curiosity in the Saturday night crowd of stirring, restless farm workers in town for excitement and to spend what there was left of their week's pay. He was the only white migratory agricultural worker to be seen in the swarming, noisy cluster of people who elbowed into and out of a combination restaurant-tavern.

Strangely enough, I had seen the scrawny, unshaven little man before, months earlier, in April—in Belle Glade, Florida, as he stood on the fringe of the "loading ground" in a knot of other white "Anglo" migrants, waiting to join a crew headed up the road. He *had* joined one and it was by the oddest possible quirk of circumstances that our paths had crossed again several hundred miles to the north.

He said his name was Herbert Glenn ("Spell it with two n's!") and that he had come originally from Madison, Wisconsin. He had been on the road—and in and out of jail—for most of the past fifteen years. He had not the slightest idea where he was going next. He wore a tattered, sweat-stained baseball cap, the visor barely clinging to the crown by a few threads. Two or three buttons were missing from his double-breasted wool pin-striped suit coat, and the mismatched trousers were fastened around the waist with a necktie.

His heavy, dusty, scarred clodhoppers were several sizes too large and his tiny feet were laced tightly into them to prevent them from falling off. He had wrapped the extra length of the laces around his ankles and it was easy to believe that he had acquired the ill-fitting footwear from some unsuspecting fellow laborer who had not been aware of the acquisition.

Glenn had a nervous habit of kicking at the black earth and cinders in the roadbed between the tracks, and though he scratched himself incessantly, he seemed unaffected by the near-90-degree heat—woolen suit and pants notwithstanding.

The most distinguishing feature about the dried-up little man was the penetrating electric blue of his eyes. When he chose, infrequently, to meet an inquiring look, it was with piercing, searching suspicion. As a lone Northern white man, caught up in the mainstream of rural Southern Negro harvesters, he had long ago conditioned himself against curious inquisitors by clothing himself in brooding reserve. He was in a group of stoop workers, but he was not of it. It was his lot to remain on the edges of crowds, on the fringes of groups, viewing proceedings from a distance. Fellow workers regarded him with distrust as he did them. He was tolerated by the Negro migrants, but never accepted.

Glenn's speech was clearly not that of the rural Deep South. It was akin to none of the dialects heard in the East Coast stream. There was a faint suggestion of a Midwestern twang; and there was at the same time an overtone of at least fleeting exposure to some form of schooling, perhaps years back in the past.

In an effort to get Glenn to unburden himself of his sorrows, I mentioned that I had seen him before at the "loading grounds" in Belle Glade.

"Yeah, I was there," he declared, "back in April. Was looking around for something to do. Been working here and there all the way up the road, till I wound up here in Hightstown the first part of July. Came in with a crew leader named Walter an' I'm telling you that was the worst thing I did."

Glenn ran a grimy hand over the gray-brown stubble around his chin, spit a wad into the roadbed and continued, "Bein' a white man with a colored crew sure ain't no picnic. It's hell! I get a hard way to go from everybody—the grower, the crew, the crew leader, and more'n' anybody else, from his wife. That woman's a bitch. Runs the kitchen at the camp where I'm at and I'm always the last one to eat. I get what's left."

Glenn had picked and loaded and lifted as much as he felt he was able to in potatoes and tomatoes in central Florida, through green peppers and cabbages in the Carolinas, to fruits and berries in Maryland, and back again to potatoes and tomatoes in Jersey. He was tired and disgusted. He had no more material wealth when I stumbled across him in Hightstown, twenty-odd miles from Trenton, then he had had the first time I had seen him in April in Belle Garde near Okeechobee. His sum total was zero; his future promised nothing more.

Glenn had been a long time away from Wisconsin. He had been in and out of three or four migrant waves—from the Texas sugar-beet fields north along the West Coast to Oregon; from acres of cotton in the Mississippi Delta up through the nation's heartline to Michigan and Minnesota corn, and several times in the midst of the flow of truck vegetables along the Atlantic Coast.

"Oh, I been around," he declared, scratching under his armpits. "I seen a lot of the country, here and there, back and forth—everywhere."

His family, he said, still lived in Wisconsin, but chances were exceedingly slim that he would ever return to visit them. There remained a mother, a father, and as far as he knew, three or four brothers. He wasn't sure of the count. He had lost contact. The years and bad times had taken their toll.

"All farm people," he said. "We had our own place till the crops went bad two years in a row and we couldn't keep what little land we had. We had to find whatever else we could do. I was the oldest, so I went out on my own. Ain't been back in twenty-five years. The rest of my folks stayed behind."

It was perfectly understandable that Glenn found the going rough in the migrant stream. As a white man, he was a minority within a minority within a minority. The overwhelming majority of the transient harvesters who move along in the ebb and flow on the East Coast are American Negroes from the rural South. There are, of course, a goodly number of Puerto Ricans, a few from the British West Indies, and several thousand from Cuba and the Bahamas. But white Anglo-Saxons have long ago moved out of the Eastern stream into urban factories, food-processing plants, and other more stable industries.

Glenn had been caught in the flow and had neither the will nor the ability to drag himself out of it. He had begun his most recent trek with a crew in Pompano Beach, Florida, and remained with it as long as the crops lasted. He then moved with another band of pickers to Belle Glade, one of the principal fountainheads of the stream. From there he went to the Carolinas, and to the fruits and berries along Maryland's eastern shore. His longest hop had been to central New Jersey with a crew headed by Walter Richards. Now, broke and disgusted, dissatisfied and disenchanted with his treatment by Walter, he was ready to move again.

"Walter's wife, Mabel, is a bitch," he repeated. "She does the cooking and the stuff she puts out ain't fit for a dog. You get two or three chicken wings and some watery rice for breakfast and that's seventy-five cents. An extra slice of bread costs you ten cents. It's a dollar a meal for supper and it's worse.

"Man can't hardly live on that kind of fare, but you got to take it or starve. Walter takes it out of your pay before you see it, whether you eat that woman's cookin' or not. He sells wine for a dollar a bottle on the side. A man knows you can buy the same stuff in the liquor store for forty-nine cents. Got to have a drink out there in the woods and you buy it from the bossman or you don't drink. I got to have wine every now and then. That's the only reason I work."

By the thin, wispy man's calculations, the crew leader's contract with the tomato grower whose fields he harvested called for 25 cents for each five-eighths-bushel basket of tomatoes. Walter, in turn, paid his fifty "head" of help 12 cents a basket. When conditions were good, each picker filled 60 to 70 baskets in each eight- to ten-hour day. Of the 3,000 to 3,400 daily baskets picked by the crew, the leader's gross receipts from the grower amounted to from $400 to $450. Added to that were the profits—deducted from each worker's pay in advance—from his wife's kitchen and the 50-per-cent markup on the wine and liquor he sold on the side.

"Pickin' ain't that good every day," the little man whined. "Sometimes it rains and don't nobody make nothing. You pay for your meals just the same. But I ain't too dumb to figure out how much Walter makes when we work. The best we can do in the field on a good day is seven or eight, maybe nine dollars. And Mabel takes out a dollar and seventy-five cents every day for the meals. Ain't fit for a dog, I tell you," he declared again. "I ain't used to that kind of cookin', but I got to eat, else I'll starve."

He ran a finger, ever so gently, over a gash on his left cheek and announced, "Oh, that fellow Walter, he beats the help terrible if they don't pick them tomatoes right. He don't allow no slackin' on his job. . . . Did he beat me? Why, yes, he did, something awful. I wasn't doing nothing for him to knock me down on the ground. I was just standing there restin' a minute and he walked up and hit me right here with his fist." He pointed to the inch-long slash. "I couldn't do nothing about it. There was all of his people there. Nobody don't mess with Walter, and they don't say nothing to his wife, either. She's meaner than him. Soon as he pays me what he owes me, I'm leavin' that man's crew and get with somebody else."

The miserable little man ambled away down the railroad tracks on the way to he didn't know where. He kicked at the cinders between the tracks as he walked and the oversized shoes flopped around on his feet. The woolen suit jacket hung almost to his knees; now and then he rubbed a finger across the gash on his cheek, a memento from labor with Walter Richard's crew that he was not likely to forget.

In a vast bean field near Salem, New Jersey, a few dozen miles southwest of Hightstown, I stumbled into a personal confrontation with still another tyrannical, evil-tempered labor-crew boss, which could have led to a fist or a club "up 'side" my own head, but for reasons far different from those which saw the diminutive white "Anglo" worker from Wisconsin groveling in the dirt at Walter Richards' big feet. I had joined the crew one morning in early August when it arrived aboard day-haul buses from Philadelphia and Camden to harvest the wide expanses of snap beans under cultivation by one of the nation's leading food processors and packers. It was an immense operation, yet just a minute part of the great agricultural complex with offices in Wall Street, which had merged, absorbed, and squeezed its way into a large portion of central and southern Jersey's many thousands of acres of salad-bowl vegetables. After leaving South Philadelphia and Camden, the labor-crew buses had stopped at other small pickup stations where day-to-day field hands gathered on street corners just after daybreak to wait for a day's work—and a day's pay.

The giant farm syndicate planted 350 acres on one side of a country road not far from Salem and 250 additional acres —in more snap beans and tomatoes—on the other. The rate on the first—and only—day I worked in the long bean fields was 40 cents a hamper, each of which contained five-eighths of a bushel. On a good day, if the crop is at peak of maturity, it is possible for a field hand to pull 20 to 30 hampers in a ten- to twelve-hour day. Of the 40 cents a basket, however, the crew contractor, as his share, skimmed 10 cents a basket off the top—called the "over-ride"—for each hand brought into the field in his bus, truck, passenger car or station wagon. Simple arithmetic told me that if the bossman hauled 40 workers into the fields and each averaged 22 hampers, each earned $8.80. But out of their share came the crew boss's over-ride of 10 cents a basket, which amounted to $88.00. If he ran several buses and hauled two or three or more loads of day workers, his profits multiplied proportionately, after the operating expenses of fuel and oil and perhaps $15.00 or $20.00 a day for drivers.

It wasn't failure to fill my hampers rapidly enough with beans from the long rows which stretched, it seemed, for miles in both directions, or that I wasn't maintaining my pace alongside the middle-aged woman and her sixteen-year-old daughter in the two adjoining rows. What angered the crew chief was that I spent more time than he thought called for in questioning the woman and the girl and insisting upon answers.

"Don't bother them people," he ordered when he marched heavy-footed along my row. "You're keeping them from making their money and they don't appreciate it. Neither do I. Next time I ketch you with your nose in their business, I'm gonna knock some of them teeth out of your mouth. You won't do no talkin' after that!"

The day-work contractor's capabilities didn't seem nearly as strong as his threats and he did, indeed, catch me—and warn me—again, but the body of strategy which had served me so well in evading serious trouble in many weeks of living, working, and traveling with a dozen-odd bands of transient crop gatherers and their leaders dictated quiet compliance.

The chances of further, possibly violent clashes with the Philadelphia labor contractor mounted during the morning and midafternoon. Rather than risk head-on collision with him, I decided the best thing for me to do was withdraw. I didn't collect the $5.00 or $6.00 he owed me, but the chance to experience firsthand some of the conditions under which migrant farm workers labor, in the North and in New Jersey, was well worth the forfeiture of a few dollars. It reaffirmed all of my earlier convictions that economic slavery—indeed, conditions only a step or two removed from peonage—is not confined to the backwoods of Dixie. It exists just commuter distance from Philadelphia and Camden and Trenton; yes, even close to New York City, toward which I headed by hopping another Greyhound bus northbound from Salem.

6

"What More Do They Need?"

A roadside tavern in central Suffolk County, New York, is a gathering place every harvest season for the farm-labor crew leaders who haul "hands" up the road from the Deep South into the heart of Long Island's richly productive white-potato belt. Potato digging—and "picking up"—begins in the late summer and—depending on the progress of the crops, and the relative goodness or badness of the growing season—extends well into November. In some instances crews work the big farms as late as the weeks before Christmas, mostly stacking the sacked potatoes in warehouses and storage bins where—in the cool darkness—they await shipment to meet market demands.

Late-model luxury automobiles, their high polish and chrome trim gleaming in the light of a bright full moon, are drawn up bumper to bumper in the tavern parking lot, or angled in from the highway out front, on any given Friday or Saturday night through the summer and fall while their owners, elbow to elbow at the tavern bar, enjoy the rewards of their crew members' toil.

Big John Matthews and Wilbur (Cookie) Cook had joined a group of colleagues at the bar on a hot, humid late August evening to partake of premium whisky and seduce any available stray woman—in that order—and to compare notes on life on the road, on the season.

"I got forty-five 'head' workin' for me," Big John declared, hoisting a Scotch-and-soda highball, "an' I'm makin' three or four times more money than you. When the potatoes and tomatoes and the other things are all in, I'll have me four or five thousand dollars in my pocket. I'm goin' back to Daytona Beach an' sit on my ass till the first of the year." John was a husky six-foot-plus. He weighed fully 280 pounds and when he took a notion to drink liquor, he approached the task with considerable gusto. "Going to buy me a new Cadillac and four or five suits before I leave here," he added, "and I won't have a thing to do till the oranges and grapefruits is ready down in Dade County."

Cookie Cook would not be outdone. He bought a round for the house in his turn, stuffed a handful of coins in the phonograph, and proclaimed, "Man, I already got more money than you. My bankroll is already fat. Time I get finished what I'm doin' I'll have enough 'bread' for a Lincoln Continental and a couple of new trucks. Can't beat this business of hustlin' the crops.

"Brought about fifty-two head up here from Goulds and Perrine and along the way an' they're all makin' money for me. Didn't charge 'em a coin to bring 'em into Long Island; don't charge 'em no money to live at my camp. Got a woman who feeds 'em in the kitchen I run, an' they got a blanket and a sheet apiece. Comes payday I come into town and buy up a whole lot of wine and things. Don't charge 'em but a dollar a bottle. They can't get it no other way. Now I ask you: 'What more do they need?' "

The moist warmth grew heavier as the crowd in the tavern increased. The coin phonograph ground music out incessantly as dimes and quarters poured one after another into its hungry maws. The fat man behind the bar sweated profusely as he tried bravely to keep abreast of the orders for drinks. On the open space in front of the jukebox couples swayed and gyrated to the plaintive wail of a male singer whose "sweet thing" had stolen away with another man.

It was Big John's turn again to sound off:

"These people I got," he boomed, "don't know nothin' better. They can't do nothin' but stoop over and pick up. I learned a long time ago not to bother with no women and kids. Mostly they ain't nothin' but trouble. I got just about all men with no families at my camp, and I know how to handle every one of them. Them that don't work like I tell 'em don't get paid 'til I get ready. That way they don't give me no trouble. There's some smart ones I got to go 'up 'side' their head with a stick once in a while. Goddammit, that sure keeps 'em in line. The man I contracts with pays me to get them potatoes out of the field and he don't give a damn how I do it, jus' so it gets done. He's got to get them potatoes out of the ground on time and it's up to me to do what has to be done. I been hustlin' this business long enough to know zackley how to do the job."

The noisy boasts of the two men continued well into the night as they hurled the sixty-five-cents-a-shot premium Scotch whisky down their throats. One thing rang brutally clear:

The illiterate, unskilled migrant farm worker exists to be cheated, overworked, underpaid, and exploited for work honestly done. He is dealt with as a commodity, a chattel, a piece of impersonal machinery necessary in the harvest of crops. The fact that he is also a human being is often tragically lost sight of in the process. It is the role of the crew leader to function as the agent of the employer, but there are no union shop stewards or business agents to represent the laborer and bargain in his behalf. The body of minimal laws designed to govern the operations of crew leaders are chronically, purposefully ignored, frequently with the knowledge and approval of farmer-employers and just as frequently with the tacit permissiveness of the authorities charged with their administration and enforcement.

At a shabby cluster of shanties near Aquebogue, Long Island, just north of Riverhead, the Suffolk county seat, I found a crew of 25 men at a grading and packing plant.

The crew leader's registration certificate, required by State Labor Department regulations, was properly posted on the commissary wall. A price list also was posted as prescribed by law. Lodging was listed as $4.00 per week per worker and board at $12.00 weekly, including 19 meals, or 75 cents a meal if purchased separately. The prevailing wage rate was $1.00 an hour for labor around the grading establishment, though neither state nor federal wage laws apply to food-processing employees.

While it was near the peak of the season in the potato harvest, less than half the crew was at work. One of the laborers explained that potatoes were trucked to the grader from surrounding fields. As no trucks had arrived during the working hours, there simply was no work to be done. The grader machinery had been halted and though the entire crew of 25 was ready, willing, and able to work—and available at the work location on the employer's request—they were not being paid for "down" time. Some of the crew were busy stacking packaged potatoes on a loading ramp in preparation for shipment by railroad car; a few others were loading the sacks into boxcars lined up on a siding. The idlers lounged around the grounds awaiting some activity at the grader. Their expenses for lodging and meals continued, but their pay did not.

A single strand of Long Island Railroad track slices through a heavily wooded area a little north of Riverhead, in Suffolk County. The trackage isn't used very much, only to shunt freight cars to and from the few scattered manufacturing firms along the right of way when materials are needed or something is ready for shipment to another place. Weeds and brush have grown up between the cross-ties and there aren't many guarded vehicle crossings. You've got to be careful and look both ways when you drive across the tracks anywhere to be sure a freight train isn't highballing from either direction.

Passenger trains didn't run on the tracks and up to the middle of 1964 it was just as well. A curious rider on the way eastward on the Island from Penn Station to Bridgehampton, or Southampton, or even as far as island's end, Montauk Point, would have seen through railroad coach windows irregular rows of low, low wooden shanties, where the town's migrant farm families lived. They weren't in fact all migrants. Any inquiry of Riverhead or Suffolk County officialdom would have brought the quick disclaimer, "Those people are absolutely not migrants. Maybe they did come up here some years ago to work in the fields, but they're here all year-around now."

And that was quite true. It would be well-nigh impossible to separate the practicing migrants from the occasional migrants, the ex-migrants and the graduate migrants at any given time, without conducting a shanty-to-shanty census. It was also true that a goodly number of the raggedy-pants, bare-footed, runny-nosed children who skipped in and out of the foul-smelling dwellings had been conceived, delivered, and reared there, in uninsulated, toiletless, running-waterless hovels. They simply hadn't known any other home.

The ugly, sprawling patch of eastern Long Island was the domain of Hollis V. Warner, a tall, strong, fierce-looking man with a mouthful of gold-jacketed bicuspids. At one time he had been one of the world's leading duck breeders in a section of the country world famous for its fine poultry. The long shanties where migrants (and ex-migrants) lived had resounded not many years ago to the quacking of thousands upon thousands of broad-billed, web-footed ducklings being fattened up for the kill and eventual retailing at gourmet shops and fine restaurants.

But a combination of factors—food prices, a depressed poultry market, competition—caused Mr. Warner to step down from his lofty role as a world-renowned duck breeder. Up until 1964, however, he had not abandoned the large tract of real estate which he had sold to a New Rochelle, New York, landholder, but which he still operated on a lease-back arrangement. He divided the flimsy wood-siding coops into one-, two- and three-room units, thereby creating his own private housing development and moved people in right behind the ducks. At peak population there were some 800 persons living on two adjoining sites of which Warner was landlord. They lived in some sixty of the far-below-standard structures and paid $15.00 to $20.00 weekly rentals. There was also an assortment of privies, unidentifiable outhouses, and pigpens on the plots. They were variously known as "Tin Tops, Numbers 1 and 2," "Indian Island" and "Hollis Warner's Duck Ranch."

The tall man liked to live close to his land and he maintained a comfortable frame residence right there in the heart of his slums. He also ran a general store in a building that at one time had been a shed for processing ducks for the market. There, he sold groceries, clothing, and other merchandise so that his tenants didn't have to bother going into town. All of the tenants were Negroes. All were in the lowest-income brackets. A substantial number of the families which replaced the ducks in Mr. Warner's sheds were on public assistance rolls. One of the surprising facts that came out of a 1964 survey of Mr. Warner's slum area by the Suffolk County Department of Health was that 25 per cent of the families had lived on the site, paying rent to Mr. Warner, from six to ten years. Two infants, born in the tin-roofed, uninsulated shacks, had burned to death there in April, 1963, and later police authorities in Riverhead, the nearest sizable town, reported that sometime during the prior four years 35 fires had broken out in the buildings, resulting in six other deaths.

Mrs. Estelle Wallace, one of the long-time tenants, had put it this way, somewhat prophetically, a few years before the 1963 fire: "When the wind catches hold of one of those fires in one of these shanties one day, the whole place is going up in a cloud of stinking black smoke." She had lived in a duck coop for more than five years. "For a colored woman like me, with children, in this part of the Island there just ain't nowhere else to be found."

Another tenant, Edward Dalton, a sixty-two-year-old native of Durant, Mississippi, told a similar story. He had arrived with a migrant crew early one spring to find that the crops he had been brought in to harvest were not ready. "I left that outfit and came into the 'duck ranch.' Started working for the man who owns this place in trade for my rent—cleaning them outhouses and doing odds and ends around here like that. He don't always pay me money for the work I do; sometimes it's groceries and meat he gets from the supermarket in Riverhead after they don't want it no more.

"Sure would like to get me 'nough money together to get back to Mississippi. Won't never come back here no more."

Mr. Warner's spotlessly white grocer's smock seemed out of place in the dim, cluttered general store when I stopped in to chat with him. Crates and boxes and cartons littered the aisle, and toward the rear more cartons were stacked almost to the low ceiling. Occasionally customers who lived on the site came in for milk, or bread, or canned goods, or meat.

I asked him how his tenants were doing.

"They're all happy people here," he said grimly. "I look out for them when nobody else will. Nobody don't want these people. Some of them are on relief. I'm the only one that gives 'em a place to live. I sell 'em their food here, and sometimes they can get it on credit when they don't have the cash. Sometimes I see that they're taken care of when they're sick. What more do they need? They're all happy here. Look around for yourself and see."

I accepted Mr. Warner's invitation. I did look—and I saw. At the time of my first visit in the summer of 1961, and again in September, 1964, there was running water in only a few of the shacks and indoor toilets in almost none. The water supply, for cooking, washing, bathing, and other uses, came from several community pumps supplied by two 1,000-gallon storage tanks. Cesspools received the toilet and sink drainage in the few converted residences that had plumbing, but rainwater simply stagnated in pools around the place until it was absorbed in the sandy earth.

Tin cans, garbage, the wrecks of scavenger-looted automobiles and all manner of other debris littered the grounds. The cockroach and vermin infestation was almost beyond belief. There were no fire hydrants or other fire-fighting devices anywhere on the site, though construction of the buildings and general living conditions made them highly inflammable.

A half-naked little girl of about four hopped and skipped among the debris near Mr. Warner's general store. From the cabin where she lived with her mother, across the dirt street, came the strong, pungent odor of Southern-style cooking. The child darted and danced around the scattered, rotting lumber and rusted machinery parts. She chattered and sang to herself in obvious delight with her own game. Her playmates were a scraggly, flea-bitten mongrel, a kitten and a few chickens. Her toys: a rusty, wobbly tricycle that didn't run and a length of rope to skip. The child was enjoying herself. Clearly she was one of Mr. Warner's happy tenants.

She had been born and nursed at her mother's breast in a single room in one of the duck sheds; she slept there in a bed at her mother's side. When the roof leaked, she got wet, and on cold winter nights when heat from the kerosene stove didn't penetrate the corners of the little room, she was cold, along with her mother and her two playmates—the little mongrel and the kitten that had come along and joined in her games one day. She was happy because she didn't yet know any other way to be. Perhaps she would never know that another, far different world lay somewhere beyond the trees that surrounded the duck ranch, a world through which other folks rode on the Long Island Railroad to Easthampton and Westhampton and Southampton, even as far out as Montauk Point, then back to their comfort in the city. Perhaps the little girl would not survive long enough to learn of the things and people and places which the trees concealed from her view.

That child, the offspring of migrant parents, short-changed of the good life, was not the only one I found who had been cheated. While traveling along a country road in late August through the rich, black-soil Irish-potato acres that border eastern Long Island's north shore, I happened across two young men who were trying desperately to escape the futility of life in a tiny detachment of the army of transient harvesters.

I had driven my own car into the potato country with the intention of joining still another migrant-farm-labor crew. I found the two men walking westward along a feeder road in the Cutchogue-Peconic area, in the direction of New York City, ninety-five miles distant. They had only the clothes they wore, 12 cents in cash between them, and part of a package of cigarettes. They had left their camp near Peconic the night before because, as they explained it, "There just wasn't any way to make enough money to live."

James Washington, nineteen, and Stanley Taylor, thirty-one, had come to Peconic from rural Polk County, Florida, a month earlier to work as laborers at a potato-grading establishment. Before boarding the crew leader's bus they had been told by the boss in his recruiting sales talk that they would be paid $1.25 an hour for 50 to 60 hours of work weekly. Upon their arrival they were told that because of prevailing market conditions, and for other vague reasons, the rate was slashed by 75 cents. "You can't make a living on fifty cents an hour," young Washington said. "Why, after everything gets taken out of our pay we don't have hardly enough left to buy razor blades."

The stories the two told were so typical of the cruel swindles perpetrated against farm workers that I postponed my own plans to work with a migrant crew in the fields and drove the two to New York City. I staked them to a room for a few days and obtained additional clothing for them. Later I guided them through the routine of the State Employment Service and helped them find work at a fruit cannery in

Geneva, New York. Before seeing them off, I recorded their experiences on two hours of tape.

They had joined Jack Wilson's crew in July when he stopped his bus and trucks to refuel at a gasoline station. "He was right about the work hours," Taylor declared, "but he sure lied about what he was payin'." He said he never actually received more than $17.00 for any of the weeks he had worked with the crew. The boss had deducted $10.00 from the gross pay for the 19 meals that he had eaten—three daily from Monday through Friday, and two on Saturday and Sunday.

There was no charge for lodging for any of the crew of nearly 70, Washington said, but the leader managed to get virtually the entire payroll back through illegal hidden charges.

"And that wasn't all," Taylor said with a frown. "He took a dollar a man out of everybody's pay every week for union dues. Nobody didn't know what union it was or what the union was supposed to do for the dollar dues. We didn't sign no union cards and didn't no union people ever come around to see how we was doing. It looked like to me that Jack put every dime of that money in his own pocket, maybe to pay for the gas comin' up from Florida.

"And another thing," young Washington volunteered, "was that he got a whole lot of free workin' time from the people in his crew. We was supposed to get an hour for lunch every day, but lots of times we didn't get but only ten or fifteen minutes. There was always some kind of excuse for callin' us back to work early—or not lettin' us off 'til a little while before the lunch hour was over. We had to load and unload trucks or clean up around the grader, any little thing that had to be done, and most times he wanted things done right away."

Other tricks the crew boss used to funnel the weekly payroll back into his own pockets, the two explained, were operating and "cutting" the payday card games and selling at 100 per cent or more markup various necessities like razor blades, toothpaste, cigarettes and toilet soap.

"He didn't miss no hustlin' gimmicks," both men declared, "and he made the most out of the girls he brought around the camp on Saturday nights." "Why, them women," Taylor elaborated, "would turn eight or ten tricks on Fridays and Saturdays—at $5.00 to $10.00 each—and Jack would take half of everything they made. Some of the men would go back two or three times to see them women. Didn't make no difference 'bout the money. They didn't have nothing else to do with it anyhow, 'cept gamble. You can't gamble all the time, can you? That man, Jack, didn't miss nothing when it came to cheatin'. The timekeeper was supposed to keep track of your hours, but a whole lot of time Jack wouldn't pay you for the time that his own man had on the books. He would say to us, "Boy, you couldn't have worked that much time. I ain't goin' to pay you for but thirty hours, 'stead of forty or forty-eight.' No matter how much time we worked, lots of times the bossman jus' wouldn' pay for it all, only what he thought we ought to have.

"And he was a mean one, too," Washington related. "I seen him go up 'side a man's head with a baseball bat. This man was going with some woman in the camp and Jack didn't like it. They was in this room together one night, the man and this woman, and Jack broke down the door. He put his shoulder up against that door and pushed and the door fell right down. He beat that man across his head and back and all over his shoulders and arms. That man couldn't work for a good spell. Last time I seen him he still had knots and marks on his head—but he didn't mess with that woman no more."

The emancipated farm laborers asserted during our tape-recording session that the crew leader deducted $1.40 each from workers on paydays for Social Security, but did not ask for Social Security numbers. "He took the dollar and forty cents out of my pay every week," Washington said, "but he never asked for my Social Security number. I got it right here in my pocket, but he never asked for it. The timekeeper never asked either."

The older of the two workers said that so many deductions were made during the first week of work with Jack Wilson's crew at the potato grader near Peconic that he drew no money at all. He said he worked between 65 and 70 hours in the second week and drew a net pay—after deductions for meals, union dues, Social Security and miscellaneous—of $4.00. He drew a net pay of $7.00 for the third week and $9.00 for the fourth. Often people who worked for Jack Wilson, and migrant-farm-labor crew leaders like him, end the week—or even the season—owing him money. During rainy periods potatoes, snap beans, corn, and other vegetables cannot be harvested. There are stoppages of work in the fields and consequently in the food-processing and packing plants. Yet expenses for food and lodging as well as other necessities continue.

"A few weeks," Taylor declared, "I ended up the week three or four dollars in the hole. There wasn't hardly no work to do 'cause of the weather and the trucks was slow comin' in. But I had to eat and buy cigarettes just the same. The man who was the timekeeper for Jack put it all down in his book that I owed the bossman."

For all of the short work weeks and delays caused by weather and slow-moving trucks, both men agreed that Jack Wilson owed them cash wages—"about two hundred dollars or more." The chances that they would recover any of it were remote. The towering, 285-pound, six-foot-three farm-labor crew leader had the cards stacked against the hired hands. He kept his own records and he handled the cash. Potato producers who wanted their fields harvested paid him a lump sum under a verbal contract and he took care of the rest. And though he could neither read nor write much more than his own name, he had "mother wit" enough to hire people who could do the necessary paperwork for him exactly the way he wanted it done.

"He ain't got no book learnin'," Stanley Taylor said in a thoughtful appraisal of the crew leader who had led him many hundreds of miles to a dead-end back-country road, "but he's sharper than most folks. He knows how to cheat, steal, and hustle like the best there is in the business; and some of the tricks he uses to get back almost all the money he pays out he invented himself. But I ain't heard of nobody who could cheat him. . . . "

Four migrant farm workers burned to death when their barracks building caught fire near Cutchogue, Long Island, in October, 1961. The flimsy wood-frame and tar-paper buildings were much like those near Peconic in which James Washington and Stanley Taylor had lived. Two infants, the children of migrant parents, burned to death in a converted duck shed near Riverhead, Long Island, in April, 1963, and a sixteen-year-old girl burned to death in a barn housing migrant farm workers near Cohocton, New York, in October, 1963.

It was because of such incidents that a half-dozen lawmakers and their staff aides gathered around a conference table in the comfort of the richly paneled, high-ceilinged Assembly Parlor at the State Capital in Albany, New York, in February, 1962. As the Joint Legislative Committee on Migrant Farm Labor, it was their responsibility, by legislative resolution, to conduct committee meetings and hold public hearings on the subject of interstate seasonal farm labor, then recommend to the State Legislature what new measures, or amendments to existing law, they thought would be necessary to improve living, working, and educational facilities for the more than 30,000 migrants expected in the state during the harvest seasons.

The Joint Committee had, indeed, complied with the Legislative resolution which created it in 1952, to

> . . . conduct public hearings within or without the state of New York, take testimony, subpoena witnesses and compel their attendance and the production of books, records, statements, documents, as may be pertinent to the study of the committee.

In preparation for the 1962 harvest seasons, the Committee met at the University Club in Albany on March 14, 1961, and spent ninety minutes mapping its over-all work programs for the on-coming season. Further responding to its legislative obligation, the Committee met again at the University Club on July 6, 1961, and this time spent two and one-half hours plotting its course toward the summer and fall harvest seasons.

Later, some Committee members spent parts of three days on a field inspection trip to twenty-two migrant-farm-labor camps in four counties in the Rochester area. A summary report of the visits said, in part: "They [the workers and their children] seemed to be quite satisfied with their way of life and no verbal complaints were received."

On a second field inspection trip to twenty-four migrant camps in four Hudson Valley counties in the vicinity of Kingston and Poughkeepsie, the Joint Committee again found living and working conditions good and morale high. Said a report of the second visit: "The workers appeared to be well satisfied with their work and living conditions. No feeling of discontent was evident anywhere in the four counties visited."

After two Committee meetings—one of ninety minutes, the other of two and one-half hours—six days of field inspections of forty-six migrant labor camps in seven upstate counties, and a two-hour public hearing at which a handful of witnesses were heard, but only briefly, the Joint Legislative Committee reached this conclusion:

> . . . while there is continuing interest on the part of many dedicated agencies in migrant matters, there seems to be a general feeling that many of the acute problems that attended the migrant in New York State a few years ago have either been resolved or, in any event, reduced.

Discontent, exploitation, violations of law and other "departures" that had been detected among migrants, the report said, resulted not from the lack of enforcement of law by those charged with such responsibility, but by a failure on the parts of the workers themselves, either through lack of knowledge or understanding, to abide by the "accepted standards of prevention and usage of facilities," or "to accept social responsibility."

The concept of the life of the migrant farm worker and

his family in America as a mean and ugly existence, just a shade short of slavery, is no longer debatable. That the nation's 400,000 to 500,000 transient harvesters—native-born American Negroes, Puerto Ricans, Mexicans, Bahamians, West Indians, American Indians, and Anglo-American whites—have been caught in the bind of economic, educational, and political depression for generations is an absolute certainty. Not even the ten-acre mule-and-plow farmer (and few of this once-hardy breed remain in today's unfaltering march toward giant syndicated, mechanized factories in the field) will deny that the occasional hired hand he puts on at season's end to help bring in the crops deserves a fair reward for his labor.

Yet the seasonal farm worker is excluded from virtually all of the benefits his industrial brother enjoys. In all of the fifty states, only Hawaii and Michigan include farm workers in effective statutory minimum-wage coverage. Puerto Rico has made a beginning in this area, with wage floors which start at 25 cents hourly and escalate to $5.50 a day. But only certain types of agricultural work is covered, largely in the sugar industry. Hawaii has fixed a $1.15 hourly wage minimum for workers employed by a grower who has twenty or more persons on his payroll in any one work week. The wage minimum does not apply, however, in the harvest of the important Hawaiian coffee crop. A few states (California, Colorado, Kansas, Oregon, Utah, Washington and Wisconsin) and the District of Columbia have minimum-wage regulations, but they apply *only* to women and children. Obviously, the District of Columbia has *no* agricultural labor problem. An administrative directive, not a law, in the State of Wisconsin, requires that women and children sixteen years of age and over be paid 75 cents an hour for farm work. Youngsters under sixteen must be paid 65 cents hourly. Administrative regulations adopted in California in 1961 set wage floors at $1.00 hourly for women and children employed on farms or in packing establishments. The same minimum applies for children over sixteen in other agricultural employment.

The State of Michigan narrowed the migrant-wage gap

in 1964, by enacting a new law which provides for a $1.00 hourly minimum, effective as of January 1, 1965. It will rise to $1.15 in 1966 and to $1.25 a year later. The bill is not nearly as good as it could have been, in the opinion of Michigan trade-movement people who guided it through the state legislature, since it covers only persons between eighteen and sixty-five years of age and only growers who employ four or more workers. Short-term migrants, in Michigan sugar beets, for example, will be excluded from statutory coverage, since the law applies only to those workers employed more than thirteen weeks.

It is a tragic commentary on the lack of enlightenment of the American community at large—and perhaps of its legislators—that all of the nation's more than 4,800,000 agricultural workers of *all* kinds are isolated by specific language of law from the benefits of the Federal Fair Labor Standards Act of 1939 (the minimum-wage law) and its subsequent amendments. It is no less tragic a commentary that powerful organized farm interests have been able to forestall the extension of federal minimum-wage laws to farm workers through the entire history of social and labor legislation in this country. While the national average hourly wage for factory workers rose to nearly $2.60 as of early 1965, the average hourly wage for *all* farm workers varied from approximately 70 cents in Mississippi to about $1.40 in Rhode Island. These estimates, arrived at by careful analysis by the U.S. Department of Labor, do not measure the hourly earnings of migrant farm workers. Because of the unstable nature of their work days and weeks; because of the varying piece, hourly, and daily rates of pay—in different fields, for harvesting different crops—and because of the very transiency of their work careers, it is virtually impossible to establish a really accurate pay scale for the seasonal agricultural worker. It is accurate to state without fear of successful challenge, however, that their annual earnings at farm work range from somewhere near $900 to about a $1200 maximum. Occasional employment at off-season, non-farm work adds a few hundred dollars to total annual income.

Yet the fruit and vegetable gatherer, and the food-packing-house laborer, and the men who operate the machinery which brings food products in, remain vital cogs in this nation's agricultural process. Without them, indeed, the harvest complex would grind to a halt. Without them many tables in many homes would be bare at the dinner hour. When the crops ripen under a benevolent sun in the lush fields of southern Florida, or along Maryland's berry-rich Eastern Shore, or in the fertile tomato-and-potato acres that border Long Island Sound, the migrant stoop laborer must be there for the harvest today, for tomorrow the sun will become destructive; it will burn the mature crops to a pulp.

To the great misfortune of the interstate harvester, he has none of the wherewithal that is necessary to wrest from employers or political organizations the living, working, and educational facilities that would lift him out of the abyss into which he has been forced by the society around him. He continues to be a classic example of powerlessness, a living symbol of economic and educational disenfranchisement. Alas, to nearly everyone's discomfort—when his mere presence is offensive to many, when time and events have rendered him unneeded and unwanted—he lacks the good grace to stuff his few belongings into his grocery-store shopping bag and vanish along with his wife and his children into that inevitable cluster of trees.

All of the grim, tawdry facts about the migrant farm worker have been thoroughly documented. His life and misery and despair are well known. It is irrefutable, for example, that the migrant continues to be the lowest and most underpaid of all wage earners in the United States today. The Department of Agriculture has reported that violations of existing child-labor laws are more flagrant among farm operators than any other employer category. It is also beyond doubt that the minimal legislation which has been enacted in the various states in behalf of the migrant has been so loosely enforced, so shabbily administered, as to render it largely ineffectual.

The Department of Agriculture every year applies its most scientific methodology and reporting machinery to calculate the wages of all farm workers. Such statistics, indeed, are gathered quarterly. Most recent 1964 figures showed the composite average hourly wage fluctuated between $.95 and $1.00. But the fluid, unstable nature of farm work on the season for the half-million-odd migrants makes it virtually impossible to plot a meaningful average-wage scale. As stated earlier in this report, he is said to earn, as of most recent 1964 estimates, between 40 and 60 cents hourly.

Yet this is a wholly unrealistic measure of the role the migrant plays—or does not play—in the American work force. He is employed fewer than 150 days a year at both farm and nonfarm occupations and at intervals between those days there are long periods of "no work" because of immature crops, crop failures, bad weather, depressed market prices for farm products, or sickness or injury. None of his work stoppages are cushioned by health or accident insurance or workmen's compensation.

An authoritative 1957 sample of migrant-farm-work patterns taken by the New York State College of Agriculture at Cornell University disclosed, as an excellent illustration, that interstate seasonal harvesters worked approximately 160 days during the previous year. The study, which has become a textbook for rural economists, also revealed that the average migrant had 201 nonproductive days during the year, 31 of which were lost as a result of slack harvest seasons, 13 because of crop failures or bad weather, with 11 days payless because of illness or injury and 5 expended in traveling from one work location to another. The balance of the time was accounted for by Saturdays, Sundays, holidays, vacations, for none of which were any wages paid.

Olaf F. Larson and Emmit F. Sharp, professor and assistant professor respectively in the Department of Rural Sociology at Cornell University College of Agriculture, sought in their 1957 study to:

1. Determine trends, work patterns and length of employment of migrants in the state.
2. Determine farm and non-farm earnings of migrants for a 12-month period.

3. Describe individual and family characteristics, use of health and educational resources, school attendance of children and workers' opinion about their experiences as part of the New York State work force.

After close scrutiny of the work experiences of 1,700 migrant workers and their families at 64 camps in 19 New York State counties, the team of Cornell rural sociologists concluded:

> If completely free choice of occupations were open, not more than one in five would prefer migratory farm work. Workers aged 45 and over, their answers probably tempered by the realities of their skills and work history, and females, were more likely than other workers to express this preference.

The two sociologists had conducted a similar study in 1953. The later survey went considerably further than did the earlier one, since it examined the extent of Social Security coverage of migrants in the state and the mechanics of interstate seasonal migrants' entering and leaving the Atlantic Coast migrant stream. It also evaluated the impact of mechanized harvest processes on the migrant-labor market, both from the worker's and the employer's point of view.

The approximately 25,000 to 30,000 migrants who labor in New York State fields or in food-processing and packing plants during harvest seasons begin arriving in March—to help in pre-harvest and planting chores for early strawberries and other fruit and vegetable crops, and to do the weeding and thinning in vineyards and orchards and in fruit and vegetable fields.

The movement builds up slowly into early June, then spurts rapidly through late August and peaks in early September. By mid-September the harvest season levels off and by late, late October or early November the great majority of out-of-state harvesters return to their home states. A few remain until mid-December, for the most part to help in grading, packaging, and storing potatoes for the winter.

New York State ranks fifth among the states in the production of all vegetables for the fresh market and for processing. It ranks fourth as a grower of white potatoes, and it stands in second place in the commercial production of apples along the Hudson Valley and the counties just south of Lake Ontario.

Because of its high food-crop production, the state is one of the largest users in the United States of migrant farm help.

The Cornell University study team found that the most fully employed category of migrants—males between ages twenty-five and forty-four—had about 235 days of paid work during the year. They were unemployed from four to five weeks.

An average 44 days were lost due to slack harvest seasons, crop failure, or bad weather. These, also, were days for which they were not paid.

Average annual earnings, the Cornell team found, varied greatly with different age groups. In New York State males aged twenty-five to thirty-four—the prime labor production spread—had an annual average wage of $1,935, or $8.26 per working day. For the same group, earnings while in New York State averaged $741.

Few workers were found who preferred farm work on the season. Uncertainty as to wages, work periods, and living conditions were the major deterrents to seeking careers as stoop laborers in orchards and vegetable fields; and migratory work was found to have the weakest hold on the younger workers who made up the bulk of the work force.

As to Social Security coverage—even though such coverage was extended in 1957 to migrants brought into the state by registered crew leaders—the workers were found to be generally uninformed or misinformed of the benefits due them under the law.

The amendment which extended Social Security benefits to migrant farm workers had a serious built-in flaw. It gave crew leaders responsibility for keeping Social Security records and many of them did not have the bookkeeping skills necessary to maintain adequate records. Only 43 per cent of the crew workers queried in 1957 reported Social Security deductions from their wages. Of non-crew workers, 88 per cent had made payments. Such workers were those who obtained work as individuals, not as members of groups traveling together. Often they found work through employment offices, sometimes by word of mouth. Frequently they were recruited on farm village street corners for day-to-day work.

As illustrations of how little New York State crew workers knew about Social Security—one of the oldest, most basic pieces of social legislation, dating back to 1935—the Larson-Sharp team found that of 455 persons questioned only two understood the program thoroughly enough to know what benefits were provided. Nearly one-third of those interviewed gave "I don't know" answers; 7 per cent expected nothing from Social Security payments and 12 per cent listed benefits which did not exist under Social Security law.

The team's exhaustive study concluded that one of the most perplexing problems concerning the migrant-farm-labor force in the State of New York was the high incidence of turnover. As some workers moved into the migrant stream, others dropped out. Clearly the migrant-farm-labor force in New York State was dominated by the short-term, inexperienced worker nearly past or past the prime production age.

Younger workers were more inclined to drop out of the stream, or go to other states to find work, because of living, working, or educational conditions.

> It is evident [the rural sociologists agreed] that a worker's experience in the current year is highly important in determining whether he will do seasonal farm work at all in the next year or, if doing so, will return to the same location.
>
> . . . whatever an employer and a community can do to provide the worker with what he considers a favorable experience will help reduce the turnover.
>
> Competitive wages and regular work are the most important factors in a good experience for the worker, but adequate housing, child-care arrangements, facilities for recreation and freedom from discrimination and from restrictive laws are also other important factors.

7

A Faint Glimmer of Hope

If Professors Larson and Sharp found a "typical" migrant farm worker in the ramshackle labor-camp shanties and the sun-washed vegetable fields of New York State in the course of their studies in 1953 and 1957, he might very well have been the same stoop-over-and-pick, straighten-up-and-carry potato-patch worker I stumbled across near Southold, Long Island.

There was a smell and feeling of autumn and season's end in the brisk late-afternoon air over the stubbled fields along the Long Island North Shore when John T. Blackwell unwound his weary, aching body and stood up in the row. It was the tail end of a punishing day and the squat, dark, sweating man had labored along with the rest of the men in his crew for the best part of ten hours at searching through the dirt for the last few hundred bags of potatoes remaining in the fields. Since he had begun working just after daybreak, stooped over on his hands and knees, John (he was called "Pore Boy," a nickname acquired at some uncertain point in the dim past of his infancy) had filled 64 burlap sacks and Long Island choice whites. Each of the dirty brown containers weighed between 80 and 100 pounds, depending upon how near to the top of the sack Pore Boy had dumped the last handfuls of potatoes. There weren't any scales out in the fields by which to gauge accurately the weight of the sacks; that would be taken care of at the grading and packaging shed, after the vegetables had been washed and sorted for size.

A full day of picking and dumping, dragging and lifting, had taken its toll on the man, yet the day's labor had not been very profitable. At 8 cents a sack, John Blackwell had earned $5.12. From that, of course, would have to come money for meals, cigarettes—maybe some new underwear if there was enough left over—and whatever other necessities he could afford. On many other occasions he had filled 75, 80, even 90 of the burlap sacks with Long Island choice whites in far less time. That was when picking was good and he felt like hustling through the rows. But for some reason, today, he hadn't felt much like scratching and grubbing the vegetables out of the black earth. He didn't feel much like doing anything. It was season's end, and Pore Boy was tired; he was tired of the kind of work that an ungracious fate had assigned to him; he was tired of the way the bossman had cheated him, over and over again, of the wages he'd earned. Further, the mechanical potato digger, which had clanked and churned through the rows earlier in the day, had not done its job well. Perhaps, like the humans who performed their roles behind it, the machine needed adjustment, or rest. Maybe, like some of the stoop-over-and-pick laborers, it was time for the machine to retire.

Because the old gasoline-powered monster's iron claws had skipped over stretches in the rows, undoubtedly without the operator's knowledge, John and the other pickers had to search through the dirt with their fingers to find the potatoes that were ready for market or storage. It made their tasks harder and it took longer to get the work done. In some places the machine in its impersonal, unseeing, nonselective manner, had chewed the potatoes into bits and pieces and the pickers had to pass over them. The unthinking machine didn't know the difference between good potatoes and bad ones; and it didn't have sense enough not to mangle the vegetables, or to say, "I'm sorry," on the many occasions when it did.

That's why the grower had to have men like John Thomas "Pore Boy" Blackwell laboring along on their hands and knees in his fields. That's also the reason the grower had to do business with the crew leaders who brought men—and some women—into the fields to do the work that the machines couldn't do.

"Be gittin' back on that truck in a day or two," John declared during a pause in his labor, "for that trip back to Florida."

He stretched to ease the kinks and knots in his muscles and continued matter-of-factly, "Ain't got a dime more now than I had when I came up here. Now, there's no more work to do."

He was thirty-eight years old and there were some 200 pounds distributed unevenly over a five-foot, nine-inch frame. The bay window that hung over his waistband got in the way all the time and the most difficult part of the potato-picking process for Pore Boy was dragging his own weight through the rows. Once he bent over it wasn't so bad, for underneath the layers of fat there *were* muscles; they had been acquired in a good many years of traveling and laboring among the crops. But when it was necessary for him to lift his own weight along with his potato sacks, he had considerable difficulty. Even in the unseasonably chill October winds off Long Island Sound he sweated freely. His shirt was soaked across the shoulders and there was an oversize V-shaped stain just under the waistline on the back of his pants—just over his meaty buttocks.

John Thomas Blackwell was more or less from Clewiston, Florida, and he could fit, perhaps as well as anyone else, into whatever mold there is for itinerant agricultural workers. He had been born in Clewiston, that's true. But he had spent time in a good many other places, some of which he also called home: Ocala, Florida, for a little while; then Daytona Beach. He had lived a year or two in Jacksonville, too, and during the World War II years he had swept floors in a mammoth chemical factory in Wilmington, Delaware. John was a farm boy though, and he made no claim to Wilmington as one of his homes. He was a restless, illiterate dreamer. He had no family to speak of; at least he didn't know where his brothers and sisters were. He wasn't even certain of how many of each there were in his family—whether new ones had arrived in his many years' absence, or whether the older ones had died or married and had children of their own. He had lost all contact with the Blackwell clan soon after leaving the few scraggly, rock-strewn acres his sharecropper parents farmed back in central Florida.

Now, at harvest's end, he could vaguely recall having begun his most recent seasonal trek after working the orange and grapefruit groves along the Florida west coast near the Gulf of Mobile. "Guess it was March or April," he said. "Don't recollect exactly. There ain't no calendars out there in the groves." Then it was up the road with various crews on various crops: potatoes and tomatoes in the northern part of the state and later into Carolina for truck crops—snap beans, cabbage, and green peppers. Here and there he picked berries, ". . . 'cause I work pretty good in the berry patches in Virginia and Maryland. Made me 'bout eight or ten dollars a day—while it lasted." He had moved from one place to another completely without plan or design. Sometimes he had hopped into an on-the-move open truck without the foggiest notion of where it was bound. At other times he had climbed into crew buses or up on the backs of migrant-crew-leaders' trucks with the rest of the gang simply because they were headed somewhere else.

"A man gets tired of stayin' in one place for very long," he announced with what he considered to be a look of profound wisdom on his brown face, "so you picks up and moves. Don't make no difference to me where I'm going to, jus' so I'm on my way."

On one trip, he recalled, he had fallen in with a band of traveling strawberry harvesters for no other reason than that he got along well with the crew boss. "He was a good man," Blackwell said, "and a lot of fun to be around. Why, we'd stay up all night tellin' lies 'till it was 'most time to go to work again in the mornin'."

There was a distinct change in Pore Boy's expression, and a drop in the tone of his voice, when he admitted somewhat sheepishly that the crew leader, Bill, had cheated him out of four days' pay after a dispute over the amount of a wage advance. Following that unfortunate experience, Pore Boy joined another group because he liked the companionship of two or three of the crew members. He stayed with that outfit for nearly a month, then paused briefly, though unwillingly, in western Maryland after getting involved in a brawl with four or five other laborers. It netted each of them five days in jail. "Wasn't my fault," John said. "Them other fellows started the fight. I was only tryin' to git out of the way. Didn't hurt me none, anyway," he declared. "I been in worse jails. The beds was good and the food wasn't bad. Anyway I needed the rest."

Yet, in the man's childlike naïveté, in his guileless susceptibility to exploitation, his unquestioning acceptance of whatever—or whoever—came his way, there was an abiding, though thoroughly fanciful vision of a better life for him somewhere else—up the road. Without ever taking conscious note of his dream, John "Pore Boy" Blackwell—born and reared on a sharecropper farm in central Florida, and educated in the labor-camp shanties and vegetable and berry fields stretching two thousand miles along the Atlantic Seaboard—sustained himself on hopes and wishes and little else. Through poverty, illiteracy, and the abuses so inherently part of his kind of existence, he never knew where his travels would take him, yet he never abandoned his dream.

Despite the grim truths of life for John Blackwell and others like him, there is hope. The public conscience has been stirred and aroused by television documentaries like "Harvest of Shame," which former U.S.I.A. chief Edward R. Murrow produced for CBS Reports in 1960, in co-operation with Fred Friendly. The National Advisory Committee for Farm Labor, based in New York City and directed by the vigilant, efficient, and untiring Miss Fay Bennett, gives its attention to legislative remedies in behalf of migratory agricultural workers. The Committee also conducts an effective fact-finding service and makes the results of its investigations available to groups, agencies, and individuals in positions to take corrective action to improve the conditions of migrant farm workers. The Bishops' Committee on Migrant Workers, a Catholic social-service agency based in Chicago, specializes in the dissemination of information on migrants. It reprints and circulates many thousands of documents, reports, and news and magazine articles concerning the transient harvester.

The Migrant Ministry of the National Council of Churches takes a direct approach in its effort to remove some of the blights of poverty and illiteracy which plague the migrant. The Ministry sends teams of missionaries into areas of heavy concentration of migrants, to conduct workshops in education, homemaking, and crafts. It also operates outpatient clinics for the treatment of ailments and disease, and holds religious services and recreational programs, Another important function of the Ministry is the sponsorship of child-care centers for migrant parents who must spend daytime hours at work in the fields and food-processing establishments.

The Migrant Ministry now operates in more than thirty-five states and employs a permanent staff of some 500 trained workers—doctors, nurses, teachers, graduate students, group worker, and sociologists. The work of professional personnel is supplemented by nearly 10,000 volunteer community workers. The year 1965 marks the forty-fifth anniversary of the Migrant Ministry.

In legislative terms, an action that the Eighty-Eighth Congress *did not* take in 1964 will have lasting impact on the wages of migratory agricultural workers, particularly in the Deep South and Southwest. Since the United States and Mexico entered into a Treaty in 1951, permission has been granted to Mexican farm workers to cross the border and seek employment wherever it could be found. In 1959, the year of maximum import of foreign farm labor, nearly a half-million such workers entered the United States. The effect of the 1951 Treaty—Public Law 78—has been that Mexican workers consistently underbid domestic workers for low-paying agricultural jobs.

The treaty was adopted to augment the American work force during the Korean Conflict. Opponents have argued that the law long ago outlived its usefulness. Organized farm interests, however, have found the cheap labor supply advantageous. Farm lobbyists fought abandonment of the law, successfully, for many years. The Congress last year permitted the law to slip into oblivion as of December 31, and though the importation of *braceros* had fallen to an average 200,000 annually in recent years, none will be permitted to enter the United States under the protection of law. One relatively immediate effect of the demise of Public Law 78 will be the loss of American dollars to the Mexican economy. But the argument is equally strong—perhaps considerably stronger—that farm-worker wages formerly paid to *braceros*—variously estimated at $40 to $50 billions annually—will remain in this country's economy. Expiration of the law is likely to generate an increase in the flow of "wetbacks," a generally derogatory term applied to Mexican nationals who cross the border illegally to find farm work in the United States, but it will be a matter of law enforcement that in a short time can be resolved.

Through the admirable vigilance and aggressiveness of the Migration Division of the Puerto Rican Department of Labor, the approximately 15,000 off-shore workers on mainland farms and in food-processing and packaging plants last year fared far better than did their mainland American counterparts. Puerto Rican workers, under Commonwealth Labor Department contracts, were guaranteed 160 hours of work for each four-week period at an hourly rate of 95 cents for a part of last year. On September 15, the contract hourly rate increased to $1.00, and, beginning with the first crops of 1965, the wage rate will climb to $1.25 hourly. A direct result of the improved wage pattern for contract workers has been improvement in the quality and performance of the workers. Many off-shore workers will return to Middle Atlantic States farm employment in 1965 for their third, fourth, and fifth years. They will bring with them skills acquired in prior satisfactory experience with employers; they will bring with them knowledgeability in languages, customs, and work habits.

Experiences of the Puerto Rican contract program, largely under the imaginative leadership of Migration Division Chief Joseph Monserrat, have proven so satisfactory that 300 to 400 such off-shore workers will be employed at harvesting California truck crops in 1965.

In addition to wage benefits guaranteed under contract to Puerto Rican workers (none of which are available to domestic farm labor) island farm workers are covered by compulsory workmen's compensation and health and accident insurance. English classes are provided for those who wish to further their education while employed on the mainland. They are housed at employer expense and furnished with bedding, cooking utensils, and silverware at supervised, regularly inspected farm-labor camps. It continues to be a source of extreme aggravation to the Commonwealth's migrant labor facility that an estimated 15,000 to 20,000 additional "walk in" farm workers not covered by contracts do not enjoy the same benefits as do those brought in under supervision. Such workers apply on their own to employers and employment offices, or answer newspaper advertisements. Many are recruited by employers or farm-labor contractors on street corners, without supervision by the Commonwealth's Migration office.

The weight of the federal government establishment has been brought into increasing play in behalf of migrants in recent years. Federal action is particularly appropriate in this area because it is only at the highest level that all segments of the farm-labor community can be brought under the protective umbrella of law. Senator Harrison A. Williams, Jr., New Jersey Democrat and Chairman of the Senate Subcommittee on Migratory Labor, is in the vanguard of a continued and persistent attack upon migrant abuses, often in the face of exceedingly strong opposition by well-financed, powerfully organized agricultural interests. The Migrant Health Act, passed by the Congress in 1962, under Senator Williams' sponsorship, authorizes up to $3,000,000 annually through 1965 for health projects in areas with substantial migrant concentration. Funds from this federal appropriation are now being used for such services as family clinics staffed by United States Public Health Service doctors and nurses. The major objective of the new law is to upgrade health services available to migrants by broadening the scope and increasing the number of existing facilities. Services are being made available to transient harvesters at their home bases, where they begin their seasonal travels from crop to crop as well as at the work locations. If such facilities had been accessible some years ago to Alonzo "Red" Fisher and his family he might have been relieved of that aching pain in his chest and the seizures which brought the look of almost intolerable pain to his face. Had clinics been available to him he might have been less a menace to others because of the red-flecked mucus which he spat into the burnt-orange dust of the Florida tomato fields. Perhaps, too, if clinical facilities had been available to the Fisher children, two of them might not have succumbed to "c'nsumption" and malnutrition and a general lack of medical attention in that backwoods labor-camp shanty in the Carolinas; and the arthritic pain that made it so difficult for Emily Fisher to get up from a chair might have been eased.

Another bill sponsored by Senator Williams and other senators, designed to limit child labor in agriculture, passed the Senate in September, 1961, but it remains stalemated in the Committee on Education and Labor in the House of Representatives. Senate field investigators found that almost half of the 200,000 to 250,000 children of migrant parents are one to four years behind in scholastic achievement. The bill as now drafted would permit children to work in agriculture outside of regular school hours, if employed by parents on the home farm, or if they are between twelve and fourteen years of age and employed within twenty-five miles of their permanent homes—with the written consent of their parents. In a report recently submitted to the Senate in support of the bill Senator Williams declared:

> The children of migratory agricultural workers are the most educationally deprived group in the nation. Their educational development is so retarded that they often fail to complete elementary school. This retardation results from the migratory way of life, which disrupts the education of the migratory child and makes it difficult for him to attend school on a regular basis. . . .
>
> The need for Federal assistance to improve the educational opportunities of [these] children is serious and widespread. . . . The inadequate education which these children receive is an inexcusable weakness in a nation which considers educational opportunity a fundamental ideal of democracy.

But the bill continues to meet strong opposition in the House, as did a companion bill which would finance special courses for adult migrants as well as for their children. The measure, again, was passed by the Senate in August, 1961, and is now pending before the Select Subcommittee on Labor of the House Committee on Education and Labor. The bill would provide financial assistance to the states under a four-part, five-year program. The federal government would supply 100 per cent of funds to educate migrant children each year for the first two years of operation. Thereafter, the cost would be shared by the federal government and the States on a 50-50 basis. Opponents of this program are concerned largely with the cost-share provision, even though the individual states would have had no financial commitment for the first two years. Anthony J. Celebrezze, Secretary of Health, Education and Welfare, supported the measure strongly. But a minority opinion rejecting it was written by Senator Barry M. Goldwater, Arizona Republican, and Senator John G. Tower, Republican from Texas.

They argued: ". . . this legislation [is] still another step in a series of attempts to interject the Federal Government into the educational systems of the United States and local communities."

A House Rules Committee hammerlock was also applied to a bill designed to set up an Advisory Council on Migratory Labor. The measure would do nothing more than establish a fifteen-member committee, representing farmers, migratory workers, social welfare interests and state governments, to advise the President and the Congress on laws and regulations relating to migrants; and to propose plans and programs directed toward meeting migrant problems effectively. The Senate passed this bill in August, 1961, and it remains pending before the Select Subcommittee on Labor of the House Committee on Education and Labor.

The Eighty-Eighth Congress did produce one major reform which will improve the lot of the itinerant crop-gatherer—The Federal Crew Leader Registration Act.

A. H. Raskin, distinguished labor writer and editorialist of the New York *Times,* pointed out in a *Times* Sunday magazine article as far back as April 24, 1960:

> Ironically, one of the places they need protection most is to curb the rapacity of the unscrupulous among their own crew leaders. These are the middlemen who link migrant and grower in a hiring system more susceptible to rackets than the outlawed "shape-up" on the New York-New Jersey waterfront. The crew leaders yank themselves out of the migrant stream by their own will to succeed. Too often their success is built on the kickbacks, jacked-up prices for food and liquor, and a monopoly over gambling and marijuana.
>
> A recent report by the Oregon Bureau of Labor indicated that the four largest Spanish-speaking labor crew contractors in the West received direct fees totalling $8,625 to

> $17,250 a week from their 5,750 crew members. And this, it was emphasized [by the Oregon Bureau of Labor], was only part of their take.

It was the lack of federal regulation of crew leaders and labor contractors (terms often used interchangeably) and less than vigorous enforcement of state laws already on the books that made possible such abuses as those I experienced as a member of Rudolph Thompson's crew in west central Florida. Bringing the crew boss under across-the-board federal legislation will aid greatly in eliminating exploitation such as that practiced by the greedy farm-labor contractor on eastern Long Island who read little more than his name, but who was shrewd enough to extract $1.00 weekly from each of his sixty-five crew members for dues to a farm-labor union which didn't exist, and to deduct $1.40 weekly from each pay envelope for Social Security payments without knowing the Social Security numbers of many of his workers.

After years of inaction, the House of Representatives passed the Senate-approved Crew Leader Registration Act on August 17, 1964, by the overwhelming vote of 343 to 7. It was signed by President Lyndon B. Johnson on September 7, 1964, and became effective as of January 1, 1965.

The measure requires the leader of ten or more migrant farm workers in interstate employment to register with the United States Labor Department. Today, under law, a crew boss, to qualify for certificates issued by the Secretary of Labor, must furnish satisfactory information concerning his conduct and method of operation as a crew boss; and must prove that he (or she) carries adequate public-liability and property-damage insurance on vehicles used in his work.

Under the law certificates can be refused or revoked for those who give false or misleading information to crew members about working or pay conditions; or who fail to comply with agreements made both with farm employers and migrant workers. Certificates can be lifted after conviction under a state or federal law relating to gambling, prostitution, alcoholic beverages or narcotics in connection with activities as a farm-labor contractor or crew leader. A last-minute amendment added in the House of Representatives before passage of this bill last year requires crew leaders to be fingerprinted to qualify for certificates. It is a safeguard designed to eliminate (or at least to identify) those farm-labor contractors with criminal records. In two states recently, nearly 10 per cent of all applicants for crew-leader licenses or renewals were found to have criminal records. Licenses were consequently revoked or denied.

Other bills passed by the Congress in 1964 and signed into law include coverage for migratory farm workers in the President's War on Poverty program—the Economic Opportunity Act of 1964—under which improvements will be made in education, child day care, sanitation, and housing. Under the law, R. Sargent Shriver, Director of the Office of Economic Opportunity, is authorized to draw money needed for these programs from a $15-million federal fund. The Act also provides for the construction of more habitable housing for migrants. Low-rent housing for transient harvesters can be built in local communities with federal assistance of up to two-thirds of construction cost. The anti-poverty law includes further provisions for improving sanitary facilities for migrants, both at their homes and at work locations. The Surgeon General of the United States, under the Act, may draw from a fund of $2.5 million to make grants to states for the improvement of such facilities for migratory farm families.

Testifying in behalf of the so-called Sanitation Facilities bill in 1962, when it was proposed as an act separate and apart from the anti-poverty legislative package, co-sponsor Senator Quentin N. Burdick gave this graphic testimony:

> I have seen myself . . . the need for this bill; I am an eyewitness . . . [in] Maricopa and Pinal Counties in Arizona . . . . What I saw on that trip, in many of those camps, was very disturbing to say the least. Some farms provided no sanitary facilities other than privies which were dirty, ramshackle arrangements. I remember one camp where four small outdoor privies were provided for workers.

> They were placed a few yards off a field, near an irrigation ditch and one family's dwelling unit. A more obvious health hazard would be hard to find. . . . These indecent, unhealthy, disease-breeding sanitation conditions must be eliminated.

At the same hearings, the Reverend James L. Vizzard, of the National Catholic Rural Life Conference, the Bishops' Committee for Migrant Workers and the Bishops' Committee for the Spanish Speaking, testified:

> . . . most consumers would gag on their salads if they saw these conditions, the lack of sanitary conditions, under which these [food] products are grown and processed.

Mr. Raskin pointed out authoritatively in the New York *Times* Sunday magazine article:

> A half century ago farm workers earned two-thirds as much as did factory workers. By the end of World War II the ratio had dropped to less than half. The present farm average of 80 cents an hour is barely a third of the factory average of $2.29.

Since Mr. Raskin wrote those words five years ago, the industrial average has climbed to $2.56 hourly. Though Mr. Raskin's comment remains basically valid, it is neither realistic nor meaningful to seek to arrive at an "average" hourly wage for migrants. Their work is seasonal, uncertain and subject to neither local, regional, nor national standards. The best available calculations, assembled by the United States Department of Agriculture after exhaustive investigation, fixes the current composite hourly wage rate of *all* of some 4.8 million farm workers at somewhere between $.95 and $1.00. But it is necessary, in appraising the wages of migrants, to isolate *them* from the total in order to arrive at an hourly wage. Despite the most intensive application of census methodology; despite the most scientific projection of labor-force statistics, it is still not possible to measure the number of migrants in the United States with any degree of real accuracy. The traveling green-pepper harvester is often on the move when the Bureau of the Census name-takers call every ten years; the itinerant potato-field harvester frequently is hidden away in a labor-camp shanty, the existence of which is completely unknown to bell-ringers and door-knockers.

Notwithstanding all of the difficulties involved in attempting to audit migratory agricultural workers, the consensus of government sources and religious and social service agencies are in conditional agreement that from year to year the number varies from 400,000 to 500,000, and that they earn between 40 and 60 cents hourly on the average. It makes a difference if a worker is white, nonwhite, Latin-American or West Indian. It also makes a difference if he is under the age of eighteen or past forty-five. The hourly, and annual, wage varies with the sex of the migrant and also depends on whether he travels as a family unit or alone. It is because of these variables that an accurate census is virtually impossible; for the same reasons the transient tomato-gatherer, or the interstate seasonal apple picker finds it so difficult to avail himself of the few services which have been provided for him.

Thus, the most controversial of the bills recommended by Senator Williams' Subcommittee on Migratory Labor is the provision for a minimum wage for the nation's farm workers. It is this measure, organized farm interests argue exhaustively, that will price many American food products completely out of the world market. The wage floor, as proposed, would be escalated over a four-year period: 75 cents an hour in the first year after the law is enacted; 85 cents the second, and $1.00 the third. The equivalent of the industrial minimum ($1.25 hourly as of January, 1965) would be achieved in the fourth year. Growers, food processors, packagers, even wholesalers and retailers, cry in a single, strident, insistent voice that a minimum wage for farm workers would boost the price of both food and nonfood products, as well as textiles and hard consumer goods, to prohibitive levels. The result, opponents declare, would be particularly burdensome to the consumer least able to pay higher prices. Yet, this is precisely the argument used by manufacturers in the early years of trade unionism and industrial-wage minimums, when it was claimed that the American industrial machine would be wiped out by the influx of sweatshop-produced items from abroad; the same argument was used much more recently by Middle Atlantic States farm-products producers who resisted paying guaranteed wages—and providing other employee benefits—to Puerto Rican contract workers.

The minimum wage paid contract workers has *not* led to agricultural chaos; it has *not* led to mass bankruptcies; it has *not* forced the New Jersey farm product out of the domestic or world market. Nonetheless, farm interest spokesmen remain adamant. It is an irreconcilable contradiction, they claim, to President Lyndon B. Johnson's heralded War on Poverty. They declare, further, that a minimum wage for the farm worker would, indeed, hasten his march to extinction and replacement by machines. The result, it is said: a glut of unlettered, unskilled, unequipped workers on the labor market, or on public assistance rolls.

Organized farm interests insist that what needs to be done to bring migratory agricultural workers into the mainstream of the American labor force can be accomplished on a state-by-state basis. Informed observers of the farm-labor picture rebut that this is far from the truth. It is their view that the process of putting migrants on a par with their industrial brothers, to a point where farm help enjoys the same benefits—and is rewarded to the same extent for his labor—as the factory worker will take a century to develop on a voluntary basis. By that time, says the consensus of informed opinion, it won't really matter. The hand harvester, the stoop laborer, will have been automated virtually out of existence.

It is today, however, that the migrant needs help, through federal legislation wherever such measures are called for, to enable him to climb out of the economic and cultural abyss caused by his lack of skills and education and to compete in the broader job market.

There was a lull in my travels with migrants in the early summer of 1961, and I chose to spend the time exploring another wellspring which supplies the Atlantic Coast seasonal interstate farm labor stream, in Charleston, South Carolina. It is a busy, teeming, hustling bastion of what was once the Confederate South. Trucks and buses, passenger cars and broken-down stationwagons, flow into and out of the old port city day and night, on their way up the road in the spring and summer; on their way back to Georgia, Florida, and Mississippi in the fall.

Railroad cars are lined up at every siding, waiting for loaders and hoisters to pack them with foodstuffs brought into town on trailer trucks, flatbeds, stake trucks and every other means of vehicular conveyance. The sounds of men and machines and sliding, scraping, groaning boxes and crates generates a dissonant clamor day and night at Charleston produce centers as the produce, many of them perishable in the warm Southern sun, are hastened to market. I paused for a while to listen to another determinate voice in support of substantive federal legislation aimed at breaking the stranglehold of economic depression which grips the migratory worker. The voice was that of Julius Amaker, a man who had been for more than two decades a farm agent with the United States Department of Agriculture. His was the specific assignment of working with Negro migrants in the Eastern Coastal States and his travels had taken him into countless fields and labor camps, from the citrus groves of Dade County in southernmost Florida, to the white-potato country of northern Maine. Retired, finally, from the rigors of bone-jolting rides over rutted country roads, and the discomfort of many nights in strange, hard beds, Mr. Amaker had opened an insurance office on a quiet, tree-shaded street in the better part of Charleston's Negro section.

"Yes, I know something about migrant farm workers," he said, leaning back in his swivel chair. "I've been around them a long time. Up until just a few years ago I lived and worked with them. It was my job as a Department of Agriculture farm agent to insure that what few federal laws were covering them were being enforced as much as possible. So I had to keep an eye on all parties concerned."

Seated behind the big walnut desk in his comfortable office, Mr. Amaker appeared to be a man of position and substance, but he had not always been so. "I came up here," he said, "from the British West Indies as a young boy." It was clear that he retained great pride in his ancestry and homeland. "But I'm in my sixties now," he went on, "and I've had to give up the rough life in the fields and camps—on the road." Mr. Amaker's hair and mustache and eyebrows were unusually thick and flecked with gray. He wore rimless eyeglasses and his countenance was one of mature, scholarly distinction. His manner was one of formality and poise. Now and then he turned his eyes to the impressive framed certificates that hung on the walls of his office. They proclaimed in flowery hand-lettered script that he was a licensed insurance agent, duly authorized by the officials of the State of South Carolina to look out for folks in the event of damage to their automobiles, or their real estate; or even in the event of death.

He rekindled his pipe with a wood kitchen match, deposited the burnt stub in an ash tray and unburdened himself of convictions he had nursed for a long time:

"It's the crew leaders," he declared. "They're the worst single evil in the whole lot. You asked me what's wrong with the migrant farm labor system and I'm telling you that's what I have come to believe.

"Not all of them, mind you; but most. They're the backbone of the whole process, yet some of them are the lowest possible form of humanity. The way they haul their help from one place to another is a crime against mankind. It's a shame on their souls. Then, when the help gets to a place somewhere along the road where there's gathering up to be done, they are cheated out of the few dollars they've earned and they're forced to live and travel under conditions that you and I wouldn't force upon animals.

"I'm not telling you what somebody told me. I'm telling you what I've seen and know. I spent more than twenty years working alongside these on-the-move workers, helping out the best way I could. I'm sorry to say that the efforts of one man haven't accomplished very much. You see, it's the system that's wrong. It's a shame; it's a tragedy; it's a sin on every one of our lives to permit human beings to live the way migrants do."

Though the gray-haired man had retired some years earlier from the punishing life on the road, the agony and despair he had shared with so many migrants remained unforgettably inscribed in his mind. The smells of a thousand mean, squalid labor camps was still in his nostrils and the sickness and death he had seen over and over again on the season, on many seasons, had been painfully, permanently, etched in his mind.

"It was my misfortune," he said after some thought of the old days, "to have been called by the authorities to visit the scene of an accident near here just a short time ago. A bus loaded with farm help had crashed through a retaining fence along the highway and rolled down a steep embankment. I don't know how many were killed—maybe twenty; maybe more. The authorities asked me if I had any ideas on the cause of the accident; whether I knew anything about how and why it had happened. Naturally, I couldn't tell if the driver had gone to sleep, or if the brakes had failed. Who knows if the old bus had any brakes, anyway? I could tell them, though—and I did—that the authorities themselves were the cause of the accident; they were to blame for the deaths of those farm workers, including a few children. Oh, not those particular officials of the State of South Carolina. I meant—and I still mean—officials on all levels who permit the transportation of human beings from one place to another in unsafe, unsound, uninspected vehicles. The truth of it is that the law requires cattle and hogs to be rested along the road at certain intervals. The law also requires them to be fed. There are no such laws to speak of governing the transportation of farm workers; and I believe that to be the cause of many deaths, maimings, and serious injuries. It has happened before, many times. It will happen again."

Slowly, belatedly, meaningful steps are being taken in various states to improve the lot of some half-million forgotten farm people. New Jersey can be credited with many firsts in the development of remedial regulations and techniques. It established a Migrant Labor Board in 1945, to co-ordinate the responsibilities in the migrant area of several agencies concerned with an important segment of the work force in a highly agricultural state. Departments assembled and centrally directed by the Board include Agriculture, Conservation and Economic Development, Education, Health, Institutions and Agencies, Labor and Industry and Law and Public Safety (State Troopers).

In 1948, for example, Puerto Rican contract workers were introduced in the New Jersey farm labor force under Migrant Labor Board supervision. During that year some 1,500 off-shore workers earned approximately $500,000 in total wages. New Jersey farm production, and along with it, farm-labor income, have come a long way in seventeen years. Foodstuffs were worth $250 millions in 1964, and at the peak employment periods employed more than 25,000 persons, including some 6,000 interstate migrants, largely from the Rural South, and more than 8,000 Puerto Ricans under contract.

With the increasing number of Puerto Rican workers coming to the mainland for farm work—and the intensive efforts of the Commonwealth's Migration Divison, specifically of its chief, Joseph Monserrat—has come greatly improved living conditions. The Glassboro Service Association, the largest organization of grower-employers in the State of New Jersey, has maintained a labor camp since 1948. In the past several years, upwards of 10,000 workers had been housed during harvest seasons at the Glassboro facility. The employees had access to an infirmary, professional medical attention, a Catholic chaplain with a mobile chapel, and the services of bilingual field workers traveling in two-way-radio-equipped vehicles. If a complaint, or an accident, occurred in the field, aid was rushed to the scene in minutes.

The Garden State is proudest of all of its rapidly growing

summer-school program for migrant children. The state operated a dozen such schools in 1964, and provided instruction for nearly 500 youngsters who otherwise would not have had formal classroom exposure at a time when their parents were employed in the fields or food-processing establishments. A greater number of such educational facilities are planned for the future. Voluntary groups have also directed an increasing amount of attention toward migrants. It is not accidental that a substantial amount of voluntary activity in this area has sprung from the fact that New Jersey Senator Williams chairs the Senate Subcommittee on Migratory Labor. He has delivered innumerable speeches on migrant problems in his state as well as in others. Many, many New Jersey residents have identified themselves with the Senator's attempts to improve the lot of the migrant. Middle Atlantic States news media also have done much, in newspapers and magazines and on radio and television to spotlight the conditions of migrants. My own newspaper articles of October, 1961, were reprinted by the tens of thousands and circulated throughout the state. The articles were reprinted separately, again by the many thousands, under sponsorship of the Bishops' Committee for Migrant Workers in Chicago, and circulated to many Catholic families and parishioners as well as to others. The dissemination of such information has not been without effect.

One of the most active voluntary groups in New Jersey is the Monmouth County Organization for Social Service. Financed by private funds, one of its first undertakings was the purchase and staffing of mobile health clinics which were sent into rural areas. Since the first traveling clinic appeared in the fields and camps in 1961, thousands of immunization injections have been given for polio, whooping cough, tetanus, and smallpox.

A public health nurse in charge of the clinic said after a period of treating and teaching small migrant children:

> It has been an opportunity and experience to be able to witness the expression of wonderment and discovery on the

faces of young children when they heard for the first time a nursery rhyme and were taught to sing simple songs.

The fact that some of them had never heard fairy tales leaves one with a feeling of pity and desire to do more.

They were confused and at times bewildered, like the little boy who was taught to say grace and thought he should repeat the prayer before every mouthful of food.

Other proof of the state's forward-looking attitude in the area of migrant farm labor is reflected in greatly intensified inspection of farm-labor camps, the updating and enforcement of building and sanitary codes, and increased activity by the State Department of Health. A massive assault on tuberculosis among migrants has resulted in the detection of hundreds of active cases of primary tuberculosis and the arrest of many more.

Yet, despite the admirable efforts of such enlightened groups and individuals, on both official and unofficial levels, the general plight of the stoop worker remains grim. The late James P. Mitchell, former United States Department of Labor Secretary who was himself at one time a New Jersey resident, said:

> Migrant workers . . . [are] caught up in a cycle of life in which poverty breeds poverty, their children are denied the educational and other opportunities to improve their status. To this end the migrant worker and his family must be given the same protection of the same beneficial type of social and labor legislation that now applies to most of his brothers.

Senator Harrison A. Williams had essentially the same view:

> Almost three decades ago we gave ourselves basic standards of minimum security: minimum wages, unemployment insurance and workmen's compensation, the right to bargain collectively, adequate provisions against child labor. All of

these things we gave ourselves. But we refused to give them to the American farm worker.

The desire for improving the living and working conditions of migrants is not shared to the same degree by everyone in New Jersey. C. H. Fields, Executive Secretary of the New Jersey Farm Bureau, gave explicit testimony before a public hearing of the House Subcommittee on Migratory Labor several years ago at the United States Courthouse in New York City. The hearings were held to air varying views on the Crew Leader Registration Act. Mr. Fields, who represented 6,000 farm families in his state, declared: "Farmers are alarmed at the provisions of the bills that have been introduced in the U.S. Senate and the House of Representatives."

Pointing out that farm production had increased by 145 per cent in the decade from 1950 to 1960, while average farm income remained below $1,000 annually, Mr. Fields added:

> Farmers are not in a position to absorb new legislation that would increase costs still further, restrict his ability to obtain labor, and sell his products in a relatively free market. . . . We do not see the need for federal legislation as long as rapid progress is being made at the state level.

Despite the poverty and ugliness in which the migrant farm worker lives and works, literally next door to affluence and plenty, some progress is being made to remove the many blights that burden him. In Suffolk County, New York, for instance, County Executive H. Lee Dennison (equivalent to the mayor of a municipality) has ordered Hollis V. Warner's private housing project completely removed from the landscape. The nearly 400-acre tract, on which some 800 persons—including many small children—lived under appalling conditions has been acquired by the County by court order. The converted duck sheds and privies have been demolished, bulldozed into heaps and burned. Nearly 200 families have been relocated elsewhere in the County, largely as a result of the efforts of Mr. Sidney E. Beckwith, chief of the Housing and General Sanitation Section of the Suffolk County Health Department. Almost every family (most of them former migrants) which remained in the County after a harvest season and found permanent employment, was relocated in roomier, cleaner, more habitable quarters and in many cases at substantially lower rental than that charged by Mr. Warner. A number of one-time migrant families found homes they liked well enough to purchase and they applied for, and were granted, mortgage financing.

The efforts of local government to remove for all time the many evils of a notorious rural slum have led to plans for reclaiming the entire duck ranch site as a public park, with picnic, recreational, and parking facilities. They have also helped to reclaim the lives of families living in Mr. Warner's duck sheds, at $15.00 to $20.00 weekly rentals, since they are now afforded a healthier environment, access to better schools, and to social services and government agencies.

Elsewhere in New York State, there is additional activity on official levels in behalf of the 35,000 transient harvesters who labor in fields and food-processing plants. Seven agencies (the Departments of Education, Health, Labor, Agriculture and Markets, Social Welfare, Motor Vehicles and State Police) working through the Interdepartmental Committee on Farm and Food Processing co-ordinate their services and facilities relating to health, housing, child care, education, working conditions and safety while at home and at work. State Health Department field workers conduct many thousands of on-the-spot, labor-camp inspections to insure that minimal standards fixed under law are followed by camp operators and growers. Immunizations are provided by the Health Department for the workers and their families against diptheria, tetanus, whooping cough, smallpox, and polio. Mobile health clinics operated by the Department are sent into farm areas to test for and treat venereal disease, tuberculosis, and other communicable diseases. Child health and maternity clinics are also operated by the State Health Department, assisted by funds made available under the Federal Migrant Health Act of 1962, one of the bills which Senator Williams helped to write into law. It is the same act against which farm lobbyists objected so strongly.

Of great significance has been the emphasis on the care and education of migrant children in New York State. During growing seasons, some 15 care centers are operated, where trained instruction and guidance are available to migrant children. Cost of these centers is underwritten 90 per cent by the state and 10 per cent by local communities, growers, or grower-employer associations. The state has taken some steps, too, to tighten regulations covering crew leaders and labor contractors—beyond what was required under the Federal Crew Leader Registration Act of 1964. New York State also requires growers using interstate farm help to register, and since 1962 has required the fingerprinting of crew leaders, with resultant screening out of a number of persons with criminal records. The State Labor Department, which has licensing authority, holds hearings in the event that complaints are filed against crew leaders, and has the power to revoke licenses or refuse applications to do business in the state.

Knottiest of all migrant problems facing officials in New York State are those involving sanitation and housing. The Joint Legislative Committee on Migrant Labor put it this way in one of its recent reports:

> There has been a marked absence of any well-defined attempt on the part of local authorities to effect regulations over housing . . . [of seasonal workers who stay on after the end of the harvests and become residents].

The report explained that official inertia often was found in areas of the state where former migrants had settled in year-round residences. Such dwellings frequently are located on the fringes of urban centers, not near enough to be included in metropolitan areas, yet close enough for easy commuting. The Joint Committee report stated further:

> A survey of these "off season" camps indicates that in many instances the housing in which they [former migrants

> who had become year-round residents] are quartered fails to come near to that which should meet necessary requirements of minimum living necessities; but for which they are paying rental charges in excess of that which prevails in the area.

The report was harshly critical of greedy landlords and unscrupulous employers:

> There still seems to be a tendency on the part of some growers to treat their labor camp as the least desirable part of the property. They still fail to respect the needs of the workers and their families and maintain an attitude of "anything that we can get away with" is all that is required. . . . Basically, he, the grower, is responsible for the introduction of the worker into the state. The welfare of these transient people only becomes the responsibility of the state when the landlord-employer fails to assume his full duty . . .

Yet, according to the Legislative Committee's analysis, the cost of housing a migrant farm worker averages approximately $2.00 weekly. "It does not appear," the group of state lawmakers concluded, "that the economic factor can legitimately be used as a reason for delaying the needed improvements in farm labor camps."

Overshadowing the complexities of personal, social, educational, and economic problems faced by the migrant farm worker in trying to support his wife and children by laboring in orchards and vegetable fields and food-processing plants along the Atlantic Seaboard, is the specter of mechanization. Often overlooked is the grim fact that there is a progressively decreasing need for the stoop worker, at the only kind of work he is equipped to perform. In New Jersey, machines are used to harvest snap beans, peas, lima beans, spinach, blueberries, cranberries, and both white and sweet potatoes. An asparagus-harvesting machine made its first appearance in the Garden State in 1963. Use of the potato-digging machine illustrates dramatically the direction and pace of mechanized agriculture. Only one such machine was in operation in the state in 1953. Ten years later nearly one hundred such pieces of equipment were clanking and churning up and down the rows. Each machine, depending upon its refinements and condition—and upon the yield of the field—replaced 20 to 25 hand gatherers. Also in New Jersey, during the mid-1960's, nearly half of the total snap-bean crop and 90 per cent of the cranberry acreage were being harvested by machines. In western New York in the same period, portable pea viners were replacing hundreds of hand workers. By 1968, agricultural economists expect that the entire pea crop will be machine harvested. Snap-bean harvesters in New York State have decreased the need for hand pickers by 25 per cent. Farm experts estimate that 2,000 stoop labor potato pickers were replaced by machines on Long Island in the ten years preceding 1964. Today, 90 per cent of the celery crop and 65 per cent of all onions in the Empire State are machine harvested.

Quite clearly the most immediate effect mechanization has had upon the agricultural migrant has been to decrease the over-all need for him. It has also required him to become far more mobile than ever before, willing to move from crop to crop, from one work location to another, on a week-by-week or day-by-day basis. The inroads of automation have increased his migrancy and at the same time increased the problems inherent in the labor of the transient harvester. Changes and improvements in mechanization and technology will undoubtedly continue over the years, even to the harvesting of highly perishable food products such as tomatoes, grapes, and cherries.

Another factor involved in mechanical harvesting is that operation of batteries of highly sophisticated, often delicate, precision machinery requires mechanical skills which interstate seasonal farm workers rarely possess. As a result, the machine operator is more often than not a member of a grower's family, or a factory-trained technician whose special skills are needed only for short periods. Then he moves along with his expertise to the next grower, in the next field. In many instances the farm-machine operator masters several different agricultural devices and becomes a year-round worker.

The development of agricultural machinery has also accelerated the merging of small family farms into giant agricultural corporations—factories in the field—since more farm machinery requires more capital investment, more research, and vastly improved farm management. Future farms will grow more on less land and employ fewer hand harvesters. The indisputable fact is that the job of the seasonal interstate migrant is moving inevitably toward extinction; yet, he will not have the skills or background or education to be absorbed in industrial employment. Clearly there is no more appropriate battleground on which to wage a "war on poverty" than the fields where the migrant stoops and grubs and gathers the nation's food crops.

Major remedial proposals in behalf of migrants (still pending before the Eighty-Ninth Congress in 1965), in addition to a minimum-wage bill and authorization of a National Advisory Council for Migratory Workers, include extension to such workers of the right to collective bargaining and further limits on child labor. Enactment of such legislation could go a long way toward bringing the migrant, his wife and his children, out of the mean, ugly hovel where he dwells.

I have experienced the misery and hopelessness of the migrant farm worker, from the Florida tomato fields where he labored stooped over in the punishing heat of a blazing sun, to the tinderbox duck shanties where he was forced to dwell on eastern Long Island. I toiled along with him in bean patches in South Carolina, and scratched potatoes out of the dirt with my fingers alongside him in south and central New Jersey. I shared wretched food—at exorbitant prices—with the hand harvester and, like him, I was cheated out of wages due me for labor honestly done. I found that despite legislative efforts in the migrant's behalf, and the praiseworthy efforts of enlightened, compassionate social-service and religious agencies, not nearly enough of real meaning has been accomplished to throw sunlight into the shadows behind the trees.

I came away angry and sick from the fields and farm-labor camps just thirty miles south of the glitter and glamor of Miami Beach. I found the same crude exploitation, the same dreadful living conditions, the same futility of life in the migrant stream, just thirty miles south of Manhattan's Times Square.

The question is: What can be done to improve the plight of the itinerant crop gatherer, whose sweat and toil—and sometimes even the blood of men like Alonzo "Red" Fisher—go into the harvest of this nation's and much of the world's food products.

These are the things that must be done:

> The farm worker must be guaranteed a fair wage for his labor, through adequate federal legislation when state and local regulations fail.
>
> He and his children, those least able to defend themselves, must be protected from exploitation by crew leaders, growers who lease for a short time his body and labor, the shipper, the packer, and the merchant—all those who regard him with so much disdain when the need for his services has ended.
>
> He and his children must be provided with adequate educational facilities, so that they can equip themselves to compete for jobs and careers with others who have that advantage.
>
> His many ailments must be treated and cured so that he can perform his honest day's work, and be assured of reward for that labor.
>
> It must be made possible for him to provide for himself and his family in comfort, peace, and dignity and in an environment which every man has a right to expect from the American Society.

The migratory agricultural worker has been hidden away in that clump of trees for so many years, for so many generations, that he often doesn't know he has certain rights and privileges in the American System.

Who can expect the sweating, hardworking, underpaid, exploited, always-on-the-move stoop laborer to demand the rights and privileges due him in a free society when he doesn't even know they exist? Historically, he has not found a place in the system; he has not been able to find his way out of the trees.

We must show him the way.